First Water

First Water: Best of Pirene's Fountain—Volume One
A Pirene's Fountain Anthology
Copyright © 2013 Glass Lyre Press.
Paperback ISBN 978-0-9840352-0-5

Editors: Ami Kaye, Mark McKay & Lark V. Timmons
Design & Layout: Steven Asmussen & Katherine Herschler
Copyediting: Royce Hamel & Elizabeth Nichols
Cover & Art: Tracy McQueen

Glass Lyre Press, LLC

All rights reserved. No part of this book may be reproduced or transmitted in any form or by any means, electronic or mechanical, including photocopying, recording, or by any information storage and retrieval system, without permission in writing from the copyright owner.

First Water
Best of Pirene's Fountain
Volume One

A Pirene's Fountain Anthology

Edited by Ami Kaye, Mark McKay & Lark V. Timmons
Design & Layout by Steven Asmussen & Katherine Herschler
Art by Tracy McQueen

Glass Lyre Press, LLC

Pirene's Fountain
A Journal of Poetry

In the lore of Greek myths naiad Pirene, grief-stricken by the death of her son Cenchrias, dissolved in a fountain of tears outside the gates of Corinth and became a spring. Pirene's fountain was sacred to the muses who drank its waters for inspiration.

At Pirene's Fountain, it is our hope that we can share of each other's knowledge, and in the spirit of Ancora Imparo (I am still learning), open our hearts and minds to inspiration.

We are privileged to bring you some of the finest poetry published in *Pirene's Fountain* during its first five years. *First Water* comprises seventy of almost five hundred poets, each one a diamond of the first water.

This anthology celebrates the diversity of life, the human condition, the beauty and complexity of language, and the ultimate springboard of poetry—the word itself.

We are endlessly grateful to our readers, the many people who shared their counsel along the way, and our enormously talented contributors. *Pirene's Fountain* and *First Water* would not have been possible without their generous and enduring gifts.

Ami Kaye
Mark McKay
Lark V. Timmons

Only one word will do. It isn't on the tip of your tongue, but you know it's not far. It's the one fish that won't swim into your net, a figure that hides in a crowd of similar figures, a domino stone in the face-down pool. Your need to find it becomes an obsession, single-minded and relentless as lust. It's a long time before you can free yourself, let it go. "Forget it," you say, and think that you do. When the word is sure you have forgotten it, it comes out of hiding. But it isn't taking any chances even now and has prepared its appearance with care. It surrounds itself with new and inconspicuous friends and faces you in a showup line in which everyone looks equally innocent. Of course you know it instantly, the way Joan of Arc knew the Dauphin and Augustine knew God. You haven't been so happy in weeks. You rush the word to your poem, which had died for lack of it, and it arises pink-cheeked as Lazarus. The two of you share the wine.

From "Stalking the Poem" by Lisel Mueller
(From *Alive Together*, LSU Press, 1995)
Published in *Pirene's Fountain*, January 2008.

Contents

Kim Addonizio
    For You — 15
    Lucifer at the Starlite — 16

Malaika King Albrecht
    Beyond the Clover Meadow — 17
    The Secret Keeper — 18

Kimberly L. Becker
    This Morning Found — 19

R. Steve Benson
    Damselfly — 20

Michelle Bitting
    Sacrament — 21
    The Sacrifice — 22

Karen Bowles
    Receding — 23

Cynthia Brackett-Vincent
    Come Morning — 24
    Hummingbirds Instead — 25

David Caddy
    Wild Swans at Stur Mill — 26
    Beauty as Melody — 27
    Tomorrow Is Another Day — 28

Jessie Carty
    Handkerchief Skin — 29

Justine Chan
    Inescapably Me — 30

Lisa J. Cihlar
    The Optimist Does Origami — 32

Beth Copeland
    Thumbnail Moon — 33
    Similitude — 34

Kelly Cressio-Moeller
    Magnolia Soulangiana (saucer magnolia) — 35

Alison Croggon
    All Souls Day — 36
    Moon — 37
    5: Intimations — 38
    Divinations — 39

Rachel Dacus
    Chopin Reigns   41

J. P. Dancing Bear
    The Magician's Assistant   42
    Music Box   43
    Night as a Love Poem   44
    A Blue Mountain at Sunset   45
    Dia De Los Muertos   46

Yoko Danno
    Fire Realm   47

Anannya Dasgupta
    From the Steps of the Jama Masjid   48

Lori Desrosiers
    Les Cigales (The Cicadas)   49

Teneice Durrant
    Glass Corset   50

Brian Fone
    Black Cockatoos   51

Amy L. George
    Zen Garden   52

Alex Grant
    The Long, Slow Drop   53
    Euclid   54
    Odin Hunts the Souls of the Dead   55
    Conquistador   56

Hedy Habra
    Broken Ladder   57
    Liberation Square   58

David M. Harris
    Nightfall   59
    Olive Alive   60

Mary Hutchins Harris
    Kyrie   61
    King Solomon's Overture   62

Melinda B Hipple
    Religioso   63
    Chimera   64
    Abstractions   65

Jane Hirshfield
    Not Moving Even One Step   66
    In A Net of Blue and Gold   67
    Pyracantha and Plum   68
    Leaving the October Palace   69
    When Your Life Looks Back   70

Paul Hostovsky
    Fledgling   72

Marcia Hurlow
    Fireflies   73
    Fish Story   74

Larry Jordan
    Translation   75
    In Spite of Doves

Robert S. King
    The Landowners of Pompeii   77

Kathleen Kirk
    Ecstasy and the Redbird   78

David LaBounty
    Jealous Poem   79

Rustin Larson
    The Emperor's Tapestry   81
    Life Documented   82
    Notebook   83
    The Collected Discography of Morning   84

Dorianne Laux
    Trees are Time   85
    Cello   86
    Heart   87
    The Shipfitter's Wife   89

Lyn Lifshin
    Blue at the Table in the Hot Sun   90
    Montmartre   91
    Nefertiti   93

Aine MacAodha
    Night Aria   94
    Mise Eire   95

Amy MacLennan
    I Close My Eyes When I Listen to Poetry   96

Dennis Maloney
    Early Morning, Hefei China   97

David McAleavey
    Including the Story about the Lake District Drunk   98

Michelle McGrane
    Čachtice   99

Catherine McGuire
    Wild Carrot   101

Steve Meador
    Witching Hour   102

Corey Mesler
- Remembering You is a Kind of Harmony — 103
- St. Valentine's Day, Morning — 104

Joseph Millar
- Love Pirates — 105
- Coming Home — 106
- Poem For Rembrandt — 107

Sue Millard
- Basil Leaves — 108

Suchoon Mo
- On The Winter Beach — 109
- An Empty Glass — 110

Jim Moore
- Two Flute Songs — 111

Karen Neuberg
- The Entire History of Your Fires — 112

Aimee Nezhukumatathil
- The Latch — 113
- The Light I Collect — 114
- Paper Person — 116

Scott Owens
- In the Cathedral of Fallen Trees — 117
- Looking For Faces in the Night Sky — 118
- Saint Sebastian's Widow — 119
- Common Ground — 122

Connie Post
- Extremities — 123

Linda Pastan
- Encore — 124
- Beethoven's Quartet in C Major, Opus 59 — 125
- Why Are Your Poems So Dark? — 126
- The Blackbirds — 127
- Shoe — 128
- Cassandra — 129

Doug Ramspeck
- Fox Lake — 131
- After That — 132

Mary Kay Rummel
- Firebird — 133
- Wounded Angel — 134

C. J. Sage
- The Weatherman's Broken Promise — 135
- Sonnet For Carryhouse and Keeper — 136
- Open House — 137

Rebecca Seiferle
    Two Versions of Bear Canyon   138
    A Broken Crown of Sonnets For My Father's Forehead   142
    The Foundling   143
    Bat in a Jar   144

John Siddique
    Fragment   145
    Adultery   146

Jeffrey Side
    Plaster Piece   147

Judith Skillman
    The Water Lily   148

Craig Colin Smith
    Song of Oak   149
    Tides   150

J.R. Solonche
    Elegy For A House Finch Killed
    Against The Window Glass   151

Joannie Stangeland
    August Is Just Long   152

Tim Suermondt
    City For The Taking   153

Maria Terrone
    Introducing the Forest to Vivaldi   154
    Words to Unpin Yourself From the Wall   155
    Artist "Anon"   156
    The Egyptian Queen Gives Death the Slip   158
    A Poet in the Customs House   159

K.J. Van Deusen
    This Wind   160

Marc Vincenz
    Black Skies   161
    Crushed Dragon Bones   162

Jane Yolen
    Color Poem For a Painter Friend   163
    The Making of Poetry   164
    Bird Recordist   165

Desmond Kon Zhicheng-Mingdé
    A Faded Postcard is a Tanka Daydream   166

Publication Credits   **168**
Contributor Notes   **172**

Kim Addonizio

For You

For you I undress down to the sheaths of my nerves.
I remove my jewelry and set it on the nightstand,
I unhook my ribs, spread my lungs flat on a chair.
I dissolve like a remedy in water, in wine.
I spill without staining, and leave without stirring the air.
I do it for love. For love, I disappear.

Kim Addonizio

Lucifer at the Starlite
—*after George Meredith*

Here's my bright idea for life on earth:
better management. The CEO
has lost touch with the details. I'm worth
as much, but I care; I come down here, I show
my face, I'm a real regular. A toast:
To our boys and girls in the war, grinding
through sand, to everybody here, our host
who's mostly mist, like methane rising
from retreating ice shelves. Put me in command.
For every town, we'll have a marching band.
For each thoroughbred, a comfortable stable;
for each worker, a place beneath the table.
For every forward step a stumbling.
A shadow over every starlit thing.

Beyond the Clover Meadow

The grey horse from the other forest
knows that a storm can steal
breath from a sleeping mouth.
She leans into the bark of the dogwood,
her back against the wet wind. Awake.
If you want to live (which I do)
learn how to lean into the forest,
bury your face into the fallen
leaves until you are the color
of loss, until you can only
be seen close up
as the reflection on a beetle's shiny back.
In the forest the angels carry
ladders of light from cloud to cloud.
One day they will lower one
through the canopy of trees
break the grey between squalls
and you will climb. You will climb
and you will sleep.

Malaika King Albrecht

The Secret Keeper

> *think how long I have known these*
> *deep dead leaves*
> *without meeting you.* —W.S. Merwin

She will cradle your handful of bees,
the fire ants, your lemon slices,
and the pale green luna moth.

She will hold your mouthful of marbles,
spent matches and kindling,
the sorrow jar, and a single key.

She will carry your field of dandelions,
the slice of borrowed sky, and your twisted
river in hers until you meet again.

Kimberly L. Becker

This morning found

a clutch of feathers, ashen
surrounded by soft down

Sacrifice under the cedar
that my dog and I discover

No body or bones; just feathers
I carefully collect in honor

of one recently flown
I clutch my find all the way home

All that remains of flight
I hold: air quivers them to life

R. Steve Benson

Damselfly

Finding a clear-winged dancer
on the fake-wood floor,
I helped her onto my finger
and carried her through
our sliding door.

Her body was lighter
than a postage stamp—
a lovely letter Returned to
Sender into the damp
morning air.

Sacrament
—for David

Sometimes when I lift the chalice
to a brother's tongue,
and tip the gleaming cup so just enough
wine flows in, the sweet red sea parting
two lip-lands like an Exodus in reverse,
my hand might accidentally brush
the other's cheek, our skins kissing briefly;
and the moment is so raw,
so vulnerable between us, anything rough
or unclean suddenly melts, passes away—
as if we have no skin,
and we are naked and new all over again,
and shame is a fruit left dangling on the vine.

The Sacrifice

I think about how you stayed up nights, Mother,
drinking coffee at your sewing machine,
finishing my Isadora Duncan costume—
diaphanous number cut from a swell of black crepe
for the mad-grief dance after her children accidentally drowned.
Remember waking to find the garment realized—
dark offering you draped across the ironing board,
fastidiously stitched seams that stroked
my just-coming curves so I'd be beautiful,
drunk in the lights of my junior high stage,
and you out there in the hushed cool of your reserved seat,
hands folded, resting now, the little bobbin of your heart
spinning inside its quiet nook while you watched me
do the hard, privileged work of feeling for both of us.

Receding

I held you as you turned
to myth
receding from my grasp
    no matter the grip
once more
out of supple reach
I held you as my heart
searched
 as if your face would appear
 behind the foggy glass
 of my bejeweled memory box
I held you as my fingers
   forgot
     their senses
       longed to stretch and turn
  another caress
  could prove we existed
I held you as you faded
     and stuttered
 no more clear voice
  yet your presence
          lingered
I held you as I moved on
     accepted
  a long cord stretched between us
    a lifeline or a sinking net
   a ladder or a binding
I held you as I looked forward
     as if I could still be held
     as if it mattered

Cynthia Brackett-Vincent

Come Morning

> *Now faith is the substance of things hoped for,*
> *the evidence of things not seen.*
> — Hebrews 11:1, KJV

September's early dusk. Kaleidoscope of light
through low trees. Starbursts become pinholes,
play tricks on the eyes. Minute by minute
each disappears. My small corner of earth gives up day.
What was there—perhaps there now—reduced
to faulty memory. Suspect memory. Nothing
to hold onto. Lights to turn on in here.

Yet this is the time the deer will come. A doe
with her fawn. In a precarious thicket between
summer & fall, she'll teach him to nuzzle
only the choicest gems—cones dark as moonless night,
seedy & oversweet. I know this. Come morning,
dew-covered & new-sunlit fruits will gleam
on the ground. Come morning, the grasses will genuflect.

Hummingbirds Instead

Inbox full, but I'm outside
chasing hummingbirds instead—
camera bouncing back & forth
each time they flit from tree to tree.
On the next bough & then the next—
needle-beak silhouette dark against sky
ruby-flash quick on blue
& suddenly I see the rest—as if my indoor eyes
had fallen away—
buttercups tall, sun-creamy yellow
& the blackberries—blackberries flowering
white like lace—
like love.

David Caddy

Wild Swans at Stur Mill

Faint churr and thrust through rush and lily
until the sluice gates temper and probe.
The water seems to stagnate and browse,
yet lower down it teems, willy nilly.

As the swans test the bank and unknown
the world revolves around them. They could take
flight or pursue other options. They ceremoniously
tread the path to the left. Water glistens, breathing.

Great soap bubbles and froth swirl. Lover after lover,
firm upon stamen and root, tight at nerve ends, edge
stubble and eroded mud to where the river softens
around islands and begins to ripple towards a charge.

Alert and undiminished perception feeds need.
A simple instinct held and executed with all its
attendant dangers from human disturbance, iodine,
hooks, nitrogen overload as the Stur current speeds.

David Caddy

Beauty as Melody

Melody stalks and stems Piddles Wood.
Her movements make you feel so good.

Edwardian timepieces sat low on the ground
and hares ran far into the century.

Cottages unaided and unbound
leapt like salmon into flat detachment.

Lead weights inscribed with two
magical words, increased rent,

or no mercy, lay heavily upon
those that fed the meadows

that fed the workers that fed
the children of their toil and bust.

My friend, Lizzie, straight and slender
as a birch, climbed so high that she could

call all our friends together and plant
our shining selves into that trembling wood

the place that makes us feel good
where beauty entreats and stuns.

Beyond the moss, ferns and bluebells
my grandchildren spore and whistle

between grass, moon carrot rust,
caul and bird's eye primrose smut,

and in their spreading they sing
so that you may step into the tender light.

David Caddy

Tomorrow Is Another Day

Tomorrow is another day
said the poet, as she filled her glass
with pistachios and heavy breasted sopranos,
and I look forward to opening a window
breathing in the space between saturated
pores and the milestone of sleep,
the logic of poaching, ritual slaughter,
our daughter of perpetual responsibility,
unable to find or cede precious gifts,
Mr Socks occupying an unmade bed,
my lover's progressive letter,
the colours and interaction of the pot,
uniting the disparate, ethnically diverse,
the silent star quitting the hospice shop,
cramps, tears at the drop of a hat,
how to proceed, the call and curl,
text and curd, keeping my wits,
concentrating on the unresolved now, overtly
sipping tea, endless bowls of cloud,
that terrible, heartbreaking stillborn loss
an unwavering commitment to love,
and my seeming clumsiness, quietness,
fruit markers, false footings,
my words slippery as eels
my unspoken desires, deft
pearls.

Jessie Carty

Handkerchief Skin
—after the poem "The Invitation" by Elizabeth Fogle

I

Handkerchief skin could be old, or fragile, something—in either case—that needs care. Wash with like colors. Even white has like.

II

Before she became a painter, she embroidered, relished the precision of stitch and back stitch, of strength made from cloth and thread. She refused the thimble, welcomed the occasional poke of needle, the cliche of suffering for her art.

III

Like a triptych, the culmination, an ancient book on display—flayed open—made from animal skin, hand sewn. Each letter individually cast in ink. Pages handled by hands in white gloves, cloth only.

Justine Chan

Inescapably Me

*"I got two six-pound little ones, because
they would look like a pair of shoes wrapped up."*
—William Faulkner, *The Sound and the Fury*

There are coffin shops in the old parts of Hong Kong,
empty and dark like garages, except for the bulks of smooth

stained wood and the spaces within. If you ask the little bald
clerk, his bare arms speckled with tiny brown islands, fanning

himself with yellowed newspaper, you could slip into one of them,
so nice and cool, and see if it will fit, with your arms folded

nicely, hands over your heart. It doesn't hurt to try
because some things are not right. I would know

because of the tight black shoes that chafed blisters
into my Achilles tendon, the long screams of ambulances

in the early blue morning, that my ye gung who swam in the ocean
every single day would die, on one of them, holding

an orange he never got to peel, my beautiful peach
faced lovebird Petey frozen in a plastic sandwich bag.

It also doesn't fit that I loved a girl, who broke my heart.
She got a dragon tattooed to her calf, called herself Ley, and I didn't

know it didn't fit to call her Ash behind the black-and-white pictures, the urns and drawers, the rice wine poured on to the black-and-white

checkered floor. Someone will mop it up later but the smoke might still burn
your eyes. It will take time, even though we flow in different time zones,

for the hurt to fleck away, like filaments of gold, pearls wrenched
from oysters too soon. I wait, the flames lick curled paper and ink,

the things we don't need but want, to breathe, shared
particles between worlds. Before I knew you,

I watched *Le ballon rouge*, by myself at the theatre, but you
were never mine and already carried away, weightless. Still,

there is a corner of my heart I saved for you.
You could come back, slip in there, and see if it will fit

before Quentin buys those lead weights like shoes
and throws himself off a bridge.

Lisa J. Cihlar

The Optimist Does Origami

She has faith that flat paper will turn into a crane. That the cranes will return from south wintering to strut the northern greening fields. She believes in yellow. Not only dandelions, but the yellow sky before tornadoes, and the yellow dog named Ned. The dog that leads his master to the best dumpsters every evening in alleys behind grocery stores and fancy restaurants to fill the wooden wagon they pull behind. It is her conviction that better is a state of mind. She trusts that Orion will return and she will stand outside on a frozen lake on the coldest night of the year with the ice cracking like rifle blasts and there will be the constellation. She will point it out to her nephew again and again and again until he can see it and follow the belt to Sirius. She will tell him it is called the Dog Star and that he can always navigate back to her with it. He falls sound asleep in the ice shanty where they fish for walleyes and the propane heater keeps it warm enough to melt the icy globes off his wool mittens. She watches his slumber and folds fortune tellers all night long to hold his dreams.

Beth Copeland

Thumbnail Moon

On the drive home
tonight, pared to the least

light of morning's leavings,
the moon, the blue, my breath

spread so thin that nothing's
left but this crone's

clipped nail, this bone
white emptiness.

Beth Copeland

Similitude

After seeking the lamp's flame
and its mate in the mirror, a moth
the color of Chinese newspapers
perches on a small picture frame,

resting on that narrow ledge
for days. Finally, it dies, light
as a dried leaf, above a print
of yellow butterflies.

Magnolia Soulangiana (saucer magnolia)

"Staring at a tree, I felt the pulse of a stone." Theodore Roethke

i
mistrustful of evergreens.
defined as deciduous was part of the appeal.
every living thing should shed their skin once a year.
one left in the back, nearly dead—perfect, i'll take it.

ii
sculptural as coral, judging by the photo.
slender bare branches promised to proffer dark purple
saucers of tea, goblets of port, depending on my mood.
if she were lipstick, i would name her violet empress.

iii
she didn't look like much. a few jaundiced ovals resembled
leaves. six years until she felt strong enough in smooth pewter
skin. long buds broke open in late winter, unexpectedly white
with pink veins, little scars, along tepals soft as well-worn suede.

iv
to be transplanted, separated from everything you've known,
takes a healthy yawn of time to revive, recover, return to normal.
offer fertile ground warmed by morning light, roots will serpent
underground, search for water, take hold. find a way to thrive.

Alison Croggon

All Souls Day

The dead have come to visit.
I don't know who they are.
They mark the glittering streets
With footsteps of rain.
The last leaves of autumn
Are their lost hands. I
Can almost hear their voices,

A rumour of wind and water.
My chest shakes like a window.
I have nothing to give them.
When I show them my hands
They turn away, disappointed.
Their eyes see through walls
To irrevocable horizons. I

Do not know their names.
Their breath beats in my arteries
Like ash, like earth, like rain
Which will never stop falling.
Their injuries taint my mouth
With a taste like blood. I
Breathe their sour bones.

I do not know what they want.
They seep into every cell
The purities of their lack.
Knowledge crumbles against them
And pours into a vast river
Where I am nameless.
The dead have come to visit

Hungry as birds in winter,
Enclosed by mortal grief
As light encloses a gesture
In darkness. I do not know
If it releases them.
Only the living are sad.
Dona eis requiem.

Alison Croggon

Moon

this moon sings
along the bones of me

each edge absolute

when my fingers open
the waters spill

words curl into air
dreaming of mouth
scythes of muscle

and in that other sky
a knife poises
its black vacuum

***

this moon pries
all secrets open

inside is black

the oyster pearl
hacked from the sea-wet
waiting lips

absolute blade
wait for me

***

in the dry country
you dream of petals
snow and milk

under your hand
the rock bleeds

under your hand the rock
is learning to sing

Alison Croggon

5: Intimations

      what is this phrase
uncurling itself
      the trees are silent
and winnow the sky
with gnarled hands
      the birds sing
but their song
only deepens the silence

Alison Croggon

Divinations

VI

You open the blue gate
in the wall of stone
and pass through the dense
birdhaunted forest

the rhododendron drops
its scarlet tongues
through the heavy green perfume
of rotting earth

and the branch which snapped
under your swinging thigh
is falling again
into the distant summer

VII

In the simple gardens
the orchards of hair and sweat

mesmeric with apple and beehum
where birdbreath tunes its delicacies

and the skeined senses tumble out their embroideries
the eyed wing, the amphibian tongue, the feathered hand

stone loosens its speech

VIII

The swallows too are bending the light
calling the blossom out of the frost
with their precise magnetic eyes
and wings of articulate hunger

out of the panic and twittering
emerges the sun and the splitting cell
shapes an eye for its mirror

and children with voices of water
carelessly inhabit the light
time for them is a bird
piping its promise on the edges of sleep

where soon the bitter ghosts will stand
like bodies of rain in the falling light
of a sunless garden

Chopin Reigns

Rain can be like Chopin, all piano strings
and syncopated pauses, geometry
of blings under wheels and rubber heels.
Sudden baptism from branches.
Drooled harmonies. On your neck, wet
strings slithering like kisses. Rings
around drops that plop into pools: ting,
ting, ting, ting. Scriabin zithering
loss up your edges, a musical soul-cling,
that cold feathering.

The Magician's Assistant

She hears the grains of the wood box singing
in this darkness that makes her realize she is
the thinnest of air, something that swords
and saw blades only wish they could cut.
She is vaporous, seeping into and out of his mind.
Not a trap door, nor a false panel, not
a mentalist's trick, not a top hat rabbit, she
does not need the whirligig eyes of Mezmer
to do what comes naturally—she is a draft
escaping through the porousness of the world.
And at night, he can hear her all around his house
pushing the leaves, playing the grass and owls,
blowing the shutters and reeding through
the window screens: her symphony of intangibility.
The Magician cannot sleep. He listens to her;
she is his muse, the oxygen to his flame, just
beyond his grasp.

J. P. Dancing Bear

Music Box

I sail my hand over her ribs,
the fine bone doors of her chest,
her house, her place of song.

Her tune—and every tune is hers—
mingles with the chilled night air;
my fingers follow the rhythm.

This door of hers keeps winter out
while exhaling summer's birdsongs,
inside I hear a sea of wheat whistling,

forest of particulated light,
gently flapping pages in a breeze
of a book I read from every day—

bible, vehicle of prayer.
O let me count another blessing
at the smooth surface of this door,

let me hear another song
from the music box of her chest—
a lullaby before this autumn sleep.

J. P. Dancing Bear

Night as a Love Poem

I am your shadow more than
myself, atmosphere without
light, transparent to stars,
this is my comet scar, my Jupiter—
red eye devoted only to your telescope.
I love it best when you reach
with your Hubble, your rockets.
What I give you best is your own
darkness bellied into a bow
pressing onto your landscapes.
Without the curve of you
I would drift into some dark matter.

J. P. Dancing Bear

A Blue Mountain at Sunset
for C.J.

you feel like half a shroud: someone who is far too intimate with clouds: they ghost through you: into blue: here where the air thins: where there is more stone than mountain top: you say there are no words for love: but forty-three words for rust: dozens for various kinds of shadow: those that darken the body: others that turn granite to indigo: so stars can find their way back into the sky: there are the words like names for the magnitude of lightning strikes: a thought fires and zig-zags along its synapse path: I call your name: it is the only word I have: for such feelings

J. P. Dancing Bear

Dia de Los Muertos
—for Jade

When we finally lie down
let peace cover our bodies,
let a fine dust and a scorpion
wander in our pelvic bones.

Our skulls will bend to touch
at the forehead, as we did
each night. Our ribs will clasp
like praying fingers,
no strand of black beads, no cross.

As our arms rest
on each others' shoulders
we will dance
that night, my Love;
we'll move across the ballroom,
glitter of the indigo sky.

Yoko Danno

fire realm

mountains are ablaze,
   a fire god awakened
      by a slash of lightning
         at the rock.

memories of minerals revived
   when the earth shakes
      revealing red chasms
         like slit eyes.

a woman stumbles to her knees
   as she senses the tremor,
      her teeth chattering
         with cold.

a shudder slides along
   the nape of her neck
      when she feels remote heat
         beneath her feet.

at the back of her eyes
   lives a salamander—
      when will it be consumed
         by its own fire?

Anannya Dasgupta

From the Steps of the Jama Masjid

Jahan Numa,
eyebrow sketched in red,
arched in perpetual
exclamation, as people,
animals, vehicles and
wares jostle beneath precarious
knots and lengths of electricity.
Before parting, I look again:
Jahan Numa,
world reflecting, divides its
pigeon blurred gaze between
the mid-day chaos of the moon
bazaar, and its own abstraction
upside down in the waterful hauz,
a liquid heart set in sandstone.

The Jama Masjid is a Mughal mosque in the heart of old Delhi. Its Persian name Jahan Numa means world reflecting. The center piece of the mosque is a water tank or a hauz, where when the light is just right, one can see the central dome of the mosque reflected perfectly. And so the mosque sits and reflects on the oldest, busiest and arguably the liveliest part of Delhi.

LORI DESROSIERS

Les Cigales (The Cicadas)

"Les cigales, les cigalons, chantent mieux que les violons".
Les Cigales —Gerard, French Art song

After sixteen years underground the bugs
emerge, their butter brown wings sticky,
climb the nearest tree to dry and harden.
They lay their eggs in wet green oak leaves,
then sing for days and days until the singing
lifts them up to swarm and die, crashing
blindly into fences, trees and homes,
before their larvae creep down trunks of trees
to find a place below the ground,
and wait another sixteen years.

At sixteen a girl is emerging
from years beneath her mother's skirts,
her butter brown eyes dewy, her gaze
not yet hardened. She lies down
beneath the oak, weeps and weeps until
the rain begins to fall, then runs inside
the house, her room door crashing shut.
She crawls beneath the bed, a place
to wait until a first lost love disperses
among the evening song of the cicadas.

Teneice Durrant

Glass Corset

No. Startled and dizzy, she asks to
take a deep breath. It's too late, mother says,
tying the pretty ribbons. Think of
yourself as a cool, shallow pool,

ornamental, and meant only to
delight and amuse. Quickly, slip the rich
dress over your head, remember how
much this means to your father, mother says.

How his good favor gained gold rope
for the trim. Quickly, hide from view
the folded flesh, compressed breasts. Let no
one hear the seams cracking. Don't betray

the broken sliver slipping between
your ribs, or how close you are to shattering.

Brian Fone

Black Cockatoos

There is never silence in this gully
and the dark encompassing green of the she-oaks
is never entirely still.

Now no negatives remain from the clear felling
which fed the sawmills seventy years ago;
the positive thrust of the straight trunks skywards
firmly asserts their continuing return.

The needles on the slope deaden a walker's footfalls,
and today any creak of branch on branch is drowned
by a constant rustle, a dry rain.

Above on nut-heavy branches sits the source.
Head quizzically cocked to observe this intruder below,
the black cockatoo questions with his upraised crest.
Beside him, his yellow faced mate looks equally askance.

The fresh light-brown of beak-crushed she-oak nuts
litters the base of the trees as the fivefold flock
bob along the branches, feast on the tiny kernels,
pausing at moments to become obsidian statues.

Then, with harsh shriekings, the flock takes off
showing glorious underbellies red or yellow,
flapping awkwardly to new casuarina stands.

Some farmer will see them cross his land and prognosticate:
Five black cockatoos—that means, in five days, rain.

Amy L. George

Zen Garden

In the center of a city
burning with the midday sun,

a garden,
a strange drop of calm

nourished my love and me,
sheltered us from the reach of chaos.

Lotus blossoms guarded silence,
only allowing dragonflies to whir through the emptiness.

Spiders spun their fragile dreams
as we wove our own through each other's fingers.

The pagoda alone heard us free our thoughts,
let them slip through flowered lips.

Shimmering koi watched them
course down the waterfalls and over stones,

swam beside them, a series of unbroken days
and promises not yet spoken.

Alex Grant

The Long, Slow Drop

A wedge of salted cantaloupe
sinking in blue agave.

A bruised peach
in a white porcelain bowl.

The heart's iambic thud,
like steps on maple floors.

Four strands of hair
in a lover's mouth.

A zinc nail sunk in bitumen.

A black-haired boy
seen in a rear-view mirror.

A plum tomato skewered
on a bamboo stave.

A Chinese flag buckled
in the monsoon's lull.

The white afternoon
turning to November dark.

Alex Grant

Euclid

—All knowledge can be derived from three things…

The strange geometry of the world
as it leans into you, pressing its circular
logic hard against your body, the tangents
and triangulations of this random arc of days
fighting for control, angled minutes and degrees
of separation shrinking and expanding like balloons
floating out to sea—the white triangled waves
reflecting clouds and stars and temporary colors—
a white breast curving like a new moon.

Alex Grant

Odin Hunts the Souls of the Dead

> *Only after Odin had plucked out an eye and thrown*
> *it into the water as a pledge, was he allowed to drink*
> *from the sacred fountain of all wit and wisdom...*
> —Norse legend

The wind rattles through the curtains, flipping
the desiccated husks of summer's flies against

the ledge—I can feel the wagon sides bounce
as it rails against the world, wailing and complaining

on its way around the sky. I look up "window"
and find Vindauga—from Old Norse—"a compound

made of wind and eye"—since once, windows contained
no glass - and I think about an old Norseman, looking

through an empty hole, wondering what he saw,
feeling the wind burn my eyes like pebbles.

Alex Grant

Conquistador

> *I said everything to them I could*
> *to divert them from their idolatries,*
> *and draw them to a knowledge of*
> *our Lord.*
> —Hernándo Cortés

Syphilis and citrus, strange bedfellows
in the jungles of Hispaniola—stranger still

in the court of Charles of Spain, bloody
emissary of the Holy Roman Church—

whose "New Spain of the Ocean Sea"
became your personal heart of darkness—

you slashed through green shoots, through
the knuckle-bruising roots and tendrils

of un-named plants and trees, glittering
cities in your mind's eye blocking out

the ragged ridges of the *Sierra de Neiba*—
the yellow crucifix a flashing lighthouse

perched above the reddest ocean in the world.

Broken Ladder

I am no longer this little boy who ran away at night to milk the moon and stars. What am I to do if the ladder is broken leaving golden threads dangling in broad daylight, braided rays of hardened light yet fine as silk spun by a silkworm, once linking me to that forever lost site of fearless joys? But I will send back the stardust I fed on for so long. Now you know why I study the Almanac, awaiting for the right day and time when wheat is ripe, reaching high into those rays of light. You know why I'm here, in the midst of this field, dressed in my Sunday clothes: I will pull these gilded chords as those of a tower bell ringing above beckoning a gift filled with the substance of dreams, wrapped with Queen Mab's veils. Don't fear it is too heavy: it weighs less than a breath or a sigh. Let the wind blow softly, watch it rise to the top with your eyes closed.

Hedy Habra

Liberation Square

In awe, I watch on my television screen
how Egyptians openly storm the streets,
walk in throngs, chant in unison their
will for change, crowding Tahrir Square.

I still remember my youth, under rigid,
military rule, when lips were sealed,
when every wall had ears, when every
corner café, every restaurant table
remembered our conversations.

That was so long ago: we chose
to leave, hearts heavy with memories.
Others got used to the status quo.

From far away, I marvel at the power
of images, when throbbing hopes
brighten ebony eyes, raise flags,
press bodies against bodies hours long,
oblivious of hunger and discomfort.

No dissonant gestures break the ebb
and flow of their unified voice,
rhythmically shaking their reclaimed
mare nostrum.

A page has been turned. Men
and women want to write letters
of freedom on their children's
foreheads, one by one,
cover the walls of their dreams
with glistening graffiti and sparkles,
erasing the memory of fear.

David M. Harris

Nightfall

In the grass, crickets sing the heat.
Behind me, dogs crunch kibble.
Above, silent bats prowl,
dark ghosts fluttering and swooping
over roof and yard,
careening through the trees and feasting,
blue-collar fliers, sweeping the air.
They draw me up,
to the Great Dog, to the Hunter,
out of the blood
that draws the mosquitoes.

David M. Harris

Olive Alive

The guidebook lied, or I misunderstood.
I thought that was the tree that Pliny saw,
and well-grown then, providing shade for all
who had their business in the Forum's courts.
Some Roman forebear put an olive tree
beside the grape and fig in Rome's old heart.
No one knows when. The tree I saw was new.
That was the one transplanted, Google says,
just sixty years ago, a stand-in for
the depths of human time.
                              Some olives from
the Empire still make oil, remembering
the wisdom of Athena and her gifts.
The last of Plato's grove was run down by
a city bus. So many promises
of oil and fruit and peace; a lot to ask.
A lot to give. To tend one tree three score
of generations can devote themselves,
enrooting them to place. The fruit and oil
and wood all drive through time to fill our needs
unconscious of our steady, vital care.
The early arborists soon learned to graft
and clone. Domesticated fruit reverts
at once to wild without our constant help.
Athena offers us abundance, peace,
and low cholesterol if we'll just tend
her trees. They speak to us from Greece and Rome,
from all the shores around the Inland Sea.
They call us to be mindful. Endless groves
or one transplanted tree will weigh the same
in our symbolic scale.
                            Make war on men,
the sages say, if you must, and enslave
your foes, but do not hurt the olive trees.

Mary Hutchins Harris

Kyrie

Blessed be the sun climbing the wall of his room, lining the sheers, blind by blind, dust motes crossing the staff of hours, minutes of shattered blue, high C sparkling the bed where he lay, chamois and sandpaper, shields against the unimagined. Blessed be the rain tapping its step-ball-change on the skylight, sending fear to slide along his arms, watering the trees he planted to shade us from too much heat, bridges of whispers that could have taught him to sing, carried eyelash to ear, until winter found its way to someone else's roots. Blessed be the unmeasured wants gargled in the roof of his mouth, watermarked in mossy green, untraced to tattered sheets, or stars that wandered alone, his everything imagined.

King Solomon's Overture

Behind the veils, sheared of pretense,
he browses among the lilies,

setting his nostrils to petals, his tongue
to the ridges of gold, one pale night

after another, to watch the temples
of pomegranate rise and fall away

like a pulse in a bed of spices, cardamom,
ginger, and a hint of soon, reflected

in the new moon, the quickening
breath of crushed apples.

Melinda B Hipple

Religioso

Ink dewdrops on a spinner's web, these notes
upon a staff ring clear, precarious
as silken thread. A winding vine denotes
which clef the maestro's Stradivarius
will choose to orchestrate the summer's heat.
Divining wind plays reeds around a marsh
while oboe charms in melodies petite.
A mimic of the grandiose or harsh
or sanguine or sublime, we stand transfixed,
transformed by timbre in the heart. Profound
the sound of Berlioz and birds when mixed:
omaggio and God's own voice are bound.

When music mimes what heaven does extol,
a note to shatter glass can mend a soul.

Melinda B Hipple

Chimera

Through the glass
a fragile image wavers
pale behind reflected skies—
mirrored moments
overlapping in a quirk of time.

A sea away
your hair falls back
revealing ice behind your eyes.

My hands reach out
to shatter glass
and break, instead,
the charm of this illusion.

Melinda B Hipple

Abstractions

He presses crumbling graphite deep; the white
of heavy texture grips each forceful line.
Suggestions of a brawny form excite
his frantic hand to grandly redefine
the flesh and blood of life upon the page.
Reality dissolves just past the muse.
Would this, a caustic piece, perhaps engage,
enrage the academe's elitist views?
No matter—his is not to fashion tripe.
Instead, he guts his soul and spills it raw
onto the wall of shadows, smears a swipe
of sore emotion drawn from passion's craw.

He dares the critic's eye to search beyond
abhorrence, grasp where truth and beauty bond.

Jane Hirshfield

Not Moving Even One Step

The rain falling too lightly to shape
an audible house, an audible tree,
blind, soaking, the old horse waits in his pasture.

He knows the field for exactly what it is:
his limitless mare, his beloved.
Even the mallards sleep in her red body maned
in thistles, hooved in the new green shallows of spring.

Slow rain streams from fetlocks, hips, the lowered head,
while she stands in the place beside him that no one sees.

The muzzles almost touch.
How silently the heart pivots on its hinge.

Jane Hirshfield

In A Net of Blue and Gold

When the moored boat lifts, for its moment,
out of the water like a small cloud—
this is when I understand.
It floats there, defying the stillness to break,
its white hull doubled on the surface smooth as glass.
A minor miracle, utterly purposeless.
Even the bird on the bow-line takes it in stride,
barely shifting his weight before resuming
whatever musing it is birds do;
and the fish continue their placid, midday
truce with the world, suspended a few feet below.
I catch their gleam, the jeweled, reflecting scales,
small dragons guarding common enough treasure.
And wonder how, bound to each other as we are
in a net of blue and gold,
We fail so often, in such ordinary ways.

Jane Hirshfield

Pyracantha and Plum

Last autumn's chastened berries still on one tree,
spring blossoms tender, hopeful, on another.
The view from this window
much as it was ten years ago, fifteen.
Yet it seems this morning
a self-portrait both clearer and darker,
as if while I slept some Rembrandt or Brueghel
had walked through the garden, looking hard.

Jane Hirshfield

Leaving the October Palace

In ancient Japan, *to travel*
meant always away—
toward the capital, one spoke only of return.
As these falling needles and leaves speak of return,
their long labors of green tired finally into gold,
the desire that remembered them into place
prepared at last to let go.
Though not for want of faithfulness—
all that once followed the sun still follows it now,
as it turns away.
The courtiers assemble their carriages, fold up their robes.
By daybreak, the soundless mountains bow under snow.

Jane Hirshfield

When Your Life Looks Back

When your life looks back—
as it will, at itself, at you—what will it say?

Inch of colored ribbon cut from the spool.
Flame curl, blue-consuming the log it flares from.
Bay leaf. Oak leaf. Cricket. One among many.

Your life will carry you as it did always,
with ten fingers and both palms,
with horizontal ribs and upright spine,
with its filling and emptying heart,
that wanted only your own heart, emptying, filled, in return.
You gave it. What else could you do?

Immersed in air or in water.
Immersed in hunger or anger.
Curious even when bored.
Longing even when running away.

"What will happen next?"—
the question hinged in your knees, your ankles,
in the in-breaths even of weeping.
Strongest of magnets, the future impartial drew you in.
Whatever direction you turned toward was face to face.
No back of the world existed,
no unseen corner, no test. No other earth to prepare for.

This, your life had said, its only pronoun.
Here, your life had said, its only house.
Let, your life had said, its only order.

And did you have a choice in this? You did—

Sleeping and walking,
the horses around you, the mountains around you,
the buildings with their tall, hydraulic shafts.
Those of your own kind around you—

A few times, you stood on your head.
A few times, you chose not to be frightened.
A few times, you held another beyond any measure.
A few times, you found yourself held beyond any measure.

Mortal, your life will say,
as if tasting something delicious, as if in envy.
Your immortal life will say this, as it is leaving.

Paul Hostovsky

Fledgling

My training wheels lie in the grass
like legs. My father stands over them,
steadying the bicycle with one hand
while with the other he beckons
with a grimy finger. A Philips head
sticks in the earth beside the severed
pair. The whole scene looks like an amputation.
I will never walk again, if I can help it—
as soon as I learn how to fly. Flying
is a little like dying, and a little
like being born. I mount the bike
which wobbles slightly in my father's grip
the way the earth wobbles in the grip
of the late afternoon sun going down
behind the huddled houses. The seat,
which is a little higher than the sun,
and the handlebars which are approximately
two stars, together form my north and south poles.
My spine is the prime meridian. My nose
sticks out over the top of the hill, on top
of the world, sniffing the air for the bottom.

Marcia Hurlow

Fireflies
—for my daughter

We had strolled by the stream and watched
the grey-brown minnows swarm in the shadows,

then we turned by the soybean field, followed
the blue clouds that swam in the dark sky

Weeds full of possum eyes, raccoon eyes,
feral eyes like quick red warnings: then

a few stray sparks lifted through the plants,
and still more until we were astronauts

set loose from our solar system, eye level
with a dozen swirling constellations.

Marcia Hurlow

Fish Story

There are stories of fish like our stories
of money, subtracting or adding misery.
There are stories of fish like our stories
of God, miraculous and wise, that require
retelling by old women, or men in robes.
When a boy casts out a line and waits
the first time by a river until the pole
genuflects to the current, and with a tug
up flies a golden fish the size of his mother's
fragile hand reaching out from her sick bed
to bless him, which kind of story is this?
Don't answer yet. As his father takes the carp
off the hook, he says it's too small to keep,
hands it to the child to throw back with a kiss.

Translation

I think I saw it; the act of it seemed
efficiently named. I was not sure
till I heard what to call it.

Descriptions added skin and ears
and wrinkles; gave it weight, made it
wobble on its axis. I saw what
you were trying to say, or at least
what you felt, while
seeing it from there. I guess

we agree on what it says, since
we both have spelled it with Zs.

Larry Jordan

In Spite of Doves

Once the winds find the mouths of flutes,
the reds get bloody and the tone turns khaki.
A light airing of valves flutter above hush,
though not quite reaching the drop of a pin.
Towards the edges of silence, a slight nudge
ripples a half breath into a skid of inhale,
piling up in sighs to bellow out some cry
that falls from treble to a mournful march
oscillating with the beat of wings.

Robert S. King

The Landowners of Pompeii

The wind seethes pumice, hurls boulders.
Streets split into four dead-end directions,
rumble of hooves, wheels, and sandals.
They who play with fire
say it is raining on the sun,
daylight spitting up in steam
darker than any alley or hiding place.

They who play with money,
lenders with gold fillings shining through,
hurry to count their change,
load it into luggage on the backs of slaves.

The guards get drunk and buy land:
They who own no boats must stay
to claim their dirt, the last thing they'll taste.

Even under fireballs falling,
the cowering shiver, cold as their futures.
The sun is a golden eye put out;
its ash whispers as it settles down, a shroud
for our bodies and whatever treasures
we take with us into night.

Kathleen Kirk

Ecstasy and the Redbird

Always, the first day
I burn, the sun and the beloved already evident

in my unprotected blush.
A redbird works so hard to unwind the dead

moonflower vine from the fence
for her nest, but she might have to give up.

Take a strand already broken, fallen,
or a thin twig, brown stem, scrap of a previous season.

She and I are nothing
alike, except in this: pale red coloring,

nesting impulse, bricolage, and making do.
I think I can say that.

I don't claim for her love or romance
or any perspective at all

on me. In that last, I am also like her.
Always, the first day, in ecstasy and burning.

David LaBounty

jealous poem

this is not
breathing
down your
back, but

forgive me
if I stare, all
because

you and I
didn't meet
electronically,
our personalities
and hopes
and dreams
weren't dictated
and painted
and paired
with little
pecks on
a keyboard
throwing
characters
on a screen
like so much
hope on a wall,

no, it was
love at
first or
second sight

so forgive me

if I think
you've been
on the computer
too long, typing
while you

bite your
bottom
lip.

Rustin Larson

The Emperor's Tapestry

He tasted no languages on his tongue,
    just sand.
        He had a certain amount of hopelessness

hanging over his eyes
    like a tapestry of white roses.
        He slept, and dreaming created

cities of echoing clay.
    He listened well, he didn't ask questions,
        he beheaded his teachers.

He had a few desperate books he was reading,
    a few wine-stained poems—
        the swan's icy fluting could rise

in his window like the sun.
    He knew when new birds stirred the pond
        to live, to eat,

or merely ignite the water and fly on.

Life Documented

but not the life lived. Near exhaustion, but
what have I done? On a whim, I take a shovel
to the yard and dig. Neighbors splay their blinds to watch me.
What is down there? I find coins and a bunch of bones.
I find an old telephone and an iron and a hit pipe some
teenager must have chucked in a panic. I find old blue
and brown medicine bottles, a cameo ring of a girl
with a garland in her hair. There are large rusted needles
and nails and hinges from cabinets.
There are porcelain knobs and shards of crockery.
There is the barrel and cylinder of an old pistol—
knife blades and tarnished silver spoons.
I dig until the moonlight fails me and I can see nothing
forever. Then I sit down on the edge
of what I am and let the wind sing in my mouth.

Rustin Larson

Notebook

The thin blue lines
upon which the words
perch—each letter
a bird on a power line.
Feed them. Spread
the sunflower and cracked
corn and millet upon
the ground. Watch
each letter be called
to you by hunger.
Hear their undisciplined
singing.
Be lost, and if you
drop bread crumbs
as you fall into the
darkness of the tall trees,
watch them be consumed
by such scarlet measures
and intervals of blue.

Rustin Larson

The Collected Discography of Morning

I went on a trip when I was 16.
Concrete boiled in ballets of paisley;
trees coiled and uncoiled, writhing, it seemed,

in ecstasy. She said I was merely seeing
time itself accelerated. I never questioned this.
A cold day I will walk

around the courthouse, admire the resin-cast
replica of Liberty, smile as people leave
the Lutheran church for their meals of shadow.

I will think
how it was years ago,
think around the rain-tight skin,

the clothes that spoke, the jeans
that fit, drum-tight, the purse of mandalas,
incantations, the money

like lost wings.
I will play the collected discography of morning,
the rain, the house carved from bone.

Dorianne Laux

Trees are Time

And their leaves fall like minutes,
eons of rings hidden at the core.

They tick like clocks in the breeze.
Birds live inside them like small beating hearts.

They watch the grass grow over their feet.
Their limbs ache when it rains.

The oldest knew the mountains when they were young,
when they had all the time in the world.

Dorianne Laux

Cello

When a dead tree falls in a forest
it often falls into the arms
of a living tree. The dead,
thus embraced, rasp in wind,
slowly carving a niche
in the living branch, sheering away
the rough outer flesh, revealing
the pinkish, yellowish, feverish
inner bark. For years
the dead tree rubs its fallen body
against the living, building
its dead music, making its raw mark,
wearing the tough bough down
as it moans and bends, the deep
rosined bow sound of the living
shouldering the dead.

Dorianne Laux

Heart

The heart shifts shape of its own accord—
from bird to ax, from pinwheel
to budded branch. It rolls over in the chest,
a brown bear groggy with winter, skips
like a child at the fair, stopping in the shade
of the fireworks booth, the fat lady's tent,
the corndog stand. Or the heart
is an empty room where the ghosts of the dead
wait, paging through magazines, licking
their skinless thumbs. One gets up, walks
through a door into a maze of hallways.
Behind one door a room full of orchids,
behind another, the smell of burned toast.
The rooms go on and on: sewing room
with its squeaky treadle, its bright needles,
room full of file cabinets and torn curtains,
room buzzing with a thousand black flies.
Or the heart closes its doors, becomes smoke,
a wispy lie, curls like a worm and forgets
its life, burrows into the fleshy dirt.
Heart makes a wrong turn.
Heart locked in its gate of thorns.
Heart with its hands folded in its lap.
Heart a blue skiff parting the silk of the lake.
It does what it wants, takes what it needs, eats
when its hungry, sleeps when the soul shuts down.
Bored, it watches movies deep into the night,
stands by the window counting the streetlamps
squinting out one by one.
Heart with its hundred mouths open.
Heart with its hundred eyes closed.
Harmonica heart, heart of tinsel,
heart of cement, broken teeth, redwood fence.
Heart of bricks and boards, heart of books stacked,
in devoted rows, their dusty spines
unreadable. Heart

with its hands full.
Hieroglyph heart, etched deep with history's lists,
things to do. Near-sighted heart. Club-footed heart.
Hard-hearted heart. Heart of gold, coal.
Bad juju heart, singing the low down blues.
Choir boy heart, heart in a frumpy robe.
Heart with its feet up reading the scores.
Homeless heart, dozing, its back against the Dumpster.
Cop-on-the-beat heart with its black billy club,
banging on the lid.

Dorianne Laux

The Shipfitter's Wife

I loved him most
when he came home from work,
his fingers still curled from fitting pipe,
his denim shirt ringed with sweat
and smelling of salt, the drying weeds
of the ocean. I would go to him where he sat
on the edge of the bed, his forehead
anointed with grease, his cracked hands
jammed between his thighs, and unlace
the steel-toed boots, stroke his ankles,
his calves, the pads and bones of his feet.
Then I'd open his clothes and take
the whole day inside me—the ship's
gray sides, the miles of copper pipe,
the voice of the foreman clanging
off the hull's silver ribs, spark of lead
kissing metal, the clamp, the winch,
the white fire of the torch, the whistle
and the long drive home.

Lyn Lifshin

Blue at the Table in the Hot Sun

give him a shot of light,
give him ragged glass
to escape thru,
black cat blues dogging
the bed

He, ok, it's you, hell bound,
in a hurry. You're pulling blue
out of the strings. Mama's got

a brand new. It's the table
in the light. Cat on the chair
with night scratching

Wind rattles the panes,
rattles gone love thru your
spine. Your baby's
changed the lock on the door

If you're still singing,
earth fills your lips

Lyn Lifshin

Montmartre

Haven't you wanted, sometimes, to
walk into some painting, start a new
life? The quiet blues of Monet would
soothe but I don't know how long I'd
want to stay there. Today I'm in the
mood for something more lively,
say Lautrec's Demimonde. I want
that glitter, heavy sequin nights.
You take the yellow sunshine.
I want the club scene that takes
you out all night. Come on,
wouldn't you, just for an evening or
two? Gaslights and absinthe, even
the queasy night after dawn. Wouldn't
you like to walk into Montmartre
where everything you did or
imagined doing was de rigueur,
pre-AIDS with the drinkers and
artists and whores? Don't be so P.C.,
so righteous you'd tell me you haven't
imagined this? Give me the Circus
Fernando, streets where getting stoned
was easy and dancing girls kick high.
It's just the other side of the canvas,
the thug life, a little lust. It was good
enough for Van Gogh and Lautrec,
Picasso. Can't you hear Satie on the
piano? You won't be able to miss
Toulouse, bulbous lips, drool. Could
you turn down a night where glee
and strangeness is wide open? Think
of Bob Dylan leaving Hibbing. A little
decadence can't hurt. I want the swirl
of cloth under changing colored lights,

nothing square, nothing safe, want to
can-can thru Paris, parting animal
nights, knees you can't wait
to taste flashing

Nefertiti

I think of her long bones,
enormous dark lake
eyes, that she would be
a beautiful ballerina,
pale with that long
swan neck. You can't
imagine her not having
beautiful perfect fingers.
Were there days, looking
out at the flood plain,
the rich black soil
and the Nile rapids,
she imagined herself free
as the sparkling water
under the blue cloudless
sky, her feet tracing
hieroglyphs, a last
S.O.S.

Aine MacAodha

Night Aria

Sounds of closing time ring out from the garage floor court
the dog groans in her sleep at the distant sound of tyres
spinning wildly in circles on the tar. Someone's idea of fun.

Reading late into the night the air gets colder just before dawn.
In the company of birdsong; they care not for time on a clock
outdo each other in a frenzy of thrills, defending territories.

They seem to snooze very little as night blends into day yet
songs of the scolding black bird in the undergrowth
sends me over the mountain to sleep; eventually.

Aine MacAodha

Mise Eire

Talk to me of bogs
of blankets on the land
talk to me of myths
you have at your command.
Tell me of Cu Chulainn
the hero hound of Ulster
The battles of the Tain Bo
and the warriors of Munster.
The progress of the firbolgs
the De danaans on the hill
remind me of our legends
of folklore through the quill.
Talk to me of forests
of flora and fauna there
talk to me of mountains
in Tyrone and in Kildare.
Tell me now of future
of equality in the land
speak to me of serenity
so the tribes can understand.

Amy MacLennan

I Close My Eyes When I Listen to Poetry

People notice. But I still close my eyes
in class, at readings. The table legs,
scarred floors, cups of coffee get in the way,
almost blur the words. Even the light
is too much. I don't want to see you,
poet speaking from the books, poet of the open mike.
Not your fingertip scanning down the page,
not your mouth. I want to be
your mouth, in the dark, your tongue
between our lips, the liquid l's and r's,
a fricative f in that inverted kiss.
I wait for your keening words, your aching words,
first spoken with no one else there, sounds
of animal or infant, fragmented, green,
pawed through and kept. Still naked.
And when you pause, I breathe as you do,
leaning toward the air in your throat,
your projected wanting, your final line.

Dennis Maloney

Early Morning, Hefei China

Men stand in front of a kiosk
reading the day's news
(news the night has brought
into day)

In the shadow of a mansion
an old woman pounds cloths
against a rock

A group of people
move as one in tai-chi
bringing the body
and city to life

In the early light
men draw long nets
along the river bottom

David McAleavey

Including the story about the Lake District drunk

When you wonder why those flaring flecks those medullary rays in quartersawn oak move us it's this you're wanting, you're wanting the soft marrow between the hard ridges marking winter's slowed growth to return and give its account of summer, of summer and the softness of the good times, the good times we bury at the end, the end of a life or a night on the town, the town now well below us since we've sweated and spat our way up, up the pass with the bench on our back which we took from the pub because we liked it, liked it because we liked it and drunk as we were still wanted to carry something forward with us to our own hut for tomorrow, tomorrow when the softness of this moment will otherwise be lost, lost unless these ribby arcs flaming across the desk sway into ghostly patterns, patterns like nebulae or fossil ripples from a long-gone sea or rings of refracted light around the moon, the moon full, full on the bench now high above Ullswater and full on the skeleton rays of the desk, the desk where we try not to lose the soft goodness where the sways from softness make patterns, patterns we see and try to keep.

Michelle McGrane

Čachtice

I

It is the winter solstice
somewhere in Transylvania.

The castle stands alone on a hill
overlooking a quiet village,
white fields either side
of a frozen river.

From a casement,
a hawk-eyed woman watches a peasant
pushed through a guard arch
onto the terrace.

Bound and gagged,
the naked girl staggers.

Voices whisper glacial tales.
Erzébet smoothes fingers
over lichened stone.

In the black-beamed passage
bats tilt in darkness.
Their mistress grows younger
by the day.

II

A dwarf with stained teeth
and cavernous eyes
kicks the serving girl to the ground.

Sinewy henchmen
surround her with buckets.

She dreams of the cottage,
her mother and sisters, and drifts,
outstretched arms paralysed.

Yew trees heave
at the edge of her sight;
the wind tastes sharp
as pine needles.

The smell of ice rises
above fortress shadows
towards the rushing light.

Catherine McGuire

Wild Carrot

Feathered ruff a green nebula
around a cage-head

of unexploded stars white fireworks
still future tense.

The unfolding covert
but discrete stages dot the field

like a history of stars:
tight bud   cage-head   burst.

It waits underground til August
has dried and scattered other weeds

it takes over where dandelion fails.
Its galaxies in the vast sheep meadows

are unexplored except
by the bees' keen astronomy.

Steve Meador

Witching Hour

It flows easily between two and three,
after bats have picked through early bird
specials at the street lamp. World and local
news has drifted downstream, plunged over
the information waterfall into a cesspool
of problems already overrunning its banks.
An average merlot sent bad vapors packing,
and parked the oak cask and light cherry
tones on the back of my tongue. The only
sound is that of the moon moving west,
until an owl kicks from its pine perch, glides
above the street, pulling a streamer of words
to be remembered and clicked onto a keyboard
before letters are swallowed by jasmine throats.

COREY MESLER

Remembering You is a Kind of Harmony

The motion of the compact disc
spinning like a planet
absorbing light to make music
calls me from my simple sleep.

I pick up the book I was reading
and it is not the book I was reading.
It is a picture of you, wearing the
night like your last prom dress.

You ask me to dance and I nod, and nod.

St. Valentine's Day, Morning

If I do not nap
I will get more done.
The world passes by,
its colorful pageantry
not yet lost to me.
The rich hours between
dawn and noon
talk to me of birds
and the music of streams.
I nod like a man en-
gaged. I nod and my
head is ponderous and lit
as if by titanic fires,
if I do not nap, my love.

Joseph Millar

Love Pirates

I follow with my mouth the small wing of muscle
under your shoulder, lean over your back, breathing
into your hair and thinking of nothing. I want
to lie down with you under the sails of a wooden sloop
and drift away from all of it, our two cars rusting
in the parking lot, our families whining like tame geese
at feeding time, and all the bosses of the earth
cursing the traffic in the morning haze.

They will telephone each other from their sofas
and glass desks, with no idea where we could be,
unable to picture the dark throat
of the saxophone playing upriver, or the fire
we gather between us on this fantail of dusty light,
having stolen a truckload of roses
and thrown them into the sea.

Joseph Millar

Coming Home

I'm fifty miles west of town,
a stranger driving this coal dust valley,
bottom land chopped out years ago,
old snow sliding into the river.
Bunch grass stabs its glittering arrows
up through the frozen gravel. I can
remember holidays like repeat episodes
of schizophrenia, furniture breaking
downstairs in the dark, everyone's head
bowed like hostages over the evening meal.
I'm passing close to the villages:
Avonmore, Saltsburg, Leechburg, Apollo.
Forgive me my history, I want to say
to these broken hills, the slow river,
it feels like it happened to someone else.
Forgive these ghost's hands bringing you nothing,
this heart filled with cobwebs and rain.

Joseph Millar

Poem for Rembrandt

It must have hurt you that winter morning
when the creditors in their stiff wool
descended like so many vultures

clucking and nodding, auctioning off
the paintings and etchings: Dürer
Rubens, Brueghel, Holbein,

then the helmets, visors, and breastplates,
antique stage props and costume finery,
your African masks, the Carpathian saddle,

Javanese shadow puppets, zithers
and gongs, even the flayed human arm
and hand afloat in a tank of gold fluid.

You buried two wives and three children
and wandered the levees in plague time,
sketchbook under one arm, past the linens

of the newly dead soaked in vinegar and
laid out to dry, while the prodigal world
kept offering itself, a blotched, aging mistress

you never abandoned. You loved what was tattered
and breaking down, the herring pier's pilings
eaten away, worn through by seaworms and ice,

or the rash corroding a soldier's cheek, paint
scabbed over, chapped by the wind: Jeremiah
musing on Zion's wreckage or St. Paul entranced

by fatigue, his sleeve mottled with lampblack.
In this late self-portrait one hooked vein throbs
below your relentless left eye.

Sue Millard

Basil Leaves

"a symbol of love in Italy; a medicinal cure for venomous
bites and the stings of scorpions"

Bella, says the waiter; basil leaves
swirl in the soup and freshen our smiles.

To drink, signora? too many miles
for wine to be our friend,
drunk enough on stained-glass sunlight
of wit and wordplay, ordinary things,
while we refuse to let years raise
their scorpion stings.

We drink warm news, till afternoon
blows chatter to the wintry street.
Our laughter shields us from the wind.
Let passing feet, privacy's thieves,
flow round goodbye,
the parting medicined
with basil leaves.

Suchoon Mo

On The Winter Beach

I walk on the winter beach
from here to there
and beyond where the beach ends
past indifferent seagulls
over beached kelps
over bleached seashells
to the sound of crushing waves
to the call of ebbing memories
I walk on the winter beach
I shall go
I must go
alone
beyond where the beach ends

Suchoon Mo

An Empty Glass

tell me not
your glass is empty
there is a happy fly in the glass
savoring wine

Jim Moore

Two Flute Songs

1
I want to become thin as a flute song
which goes into the delicate inner ear
and coils there, holding in balance the lives
of everyone I love.

2
It's late and the furnace goes full blast
filling the room like a good joke.
I read aloud, pausing for air.
If my pipe were alive
I could not hold it more lovingly.
Soon, I will make green tea
and pray that the flute song I barely hear
is not a signal for dawn
and is not a record, nor an answer
to any questions I might pose it.

Karen Neuberg

The Entire History of Your Fires

The entire history of your fires
wedges between green logs
and ashes. Stale smoke ascending
into chaos scrapes
alongside you in sleep. You've seen
desire turn
into an old woman, seen it turn into
twenty songs depicting your entire story.
Dreams caught strolling up the sides
of memory, as if memory
was nothing more than just a chimney
emptying your past
into anonymity of sky.

Aimee Nezhukumatathil

The Latch

The days before her first son arrived were spent worrying about The Latch: the perfect hold of a baby's mouth onto a breast, the scoop of lip rolling out a welcome to a river. There were books about The Latch. She read them. There were videos of The Latch. She watched them. The proper way to latch, the painful way to latch. The Football Hold. The Cradle Hold. She studied them all, with glasses on. She circled round and round like being pulled in a cart by wee goats on Coney Island. But she couldn't ever get it right. If she thought to wear her silver anklets her Indian grandmother gave her, at least there would be happy bells. Days of cold packs every three hours. Days of tucking torn cabbage leaves into her bra to cool and calm the milk. The bite of a baby is like a prawn claw on your calf. The blade of the unlucky axe that chopped down a jackfruit tree. A cut on your wrist from a broken glass bangle. A sunless forest snake. A mirror cut with a diamond pen. The second time around, with the second son, The Latch becomes a beautiful story. A whole world of skink feet and furred shoulder-blades she could cup with one hand. It will always be summer. There is a plastic pool with little sailboats tracing lazy numbers across the stretch of clouds. Someone is grilling meats. The Latch is the plum and lightning bug. The birdcall and tanned hands. The Latch is a half-closed eyelid and envelope sent across an ocean and the ocean is a bird.

                                        And The Latch is the world.

Aimee Nezhukumatathil

The Light I Collect

"The baby's foot is not yet aware it is a foot,
and would like to be a butterfly or an apple."—Neruda

If a man in China can keep ten-thousand dollars' worth
of caterpillars in a metal box underneath his bed
for medicine, then I want to collect flakes of light
for those winter months when we go a whole week

without seeing a slice of sun. The light I want to collect
is free. Can't be sold as a cure for muscle ache
or to ward off evil eye. I write this in August. It should be
illegal to talk about snow in Western New York now.

I will probably be fined. So many parts
of my newborn son are translucent: eyelids,
his slightly furry nose-tip, the small webbing between
his fingers. When I hold him in the sunshine, even his ears

glow from behind like a church window shining
a celebration within. When he is hungry, I see his feet
kick up from the side of his cradle, motoring the air
like a pumpjack in the Kansas oilfields where his father

grew up. And maybe it's the lack of sleep, but sometimes
my baby's foot feels like a hairless mouse that runs
along the edges of my shirt in search of crumbs
from my last meal. I've been nursing this boy every

two hours in the middle of a record heat wave.
Everyone in town is asleep except for my son and me
and no one even *dreams* of dreams of snow. Without
my glasses, the edge of his foot blurs even more

during those early morning hours. It shimmers
into a perfect peach sold by my favorite fruit farm
on Route 20 where the old lady who shuffles out
to measure my haul of fruit is still in her flowered

nightgown, still in her slippers, and calls me
Sugarbaby, Sugarbaby, Now Where Did I Put My Pen.

Aimee Nezhukumatathil

Paper Person

       I trace paper's origins
to ancient China, where a eunuch
in the Imperial Household collects
wasps. He watches them bounce
against oiled panes of linen, chew
mulberry wood into a pulp and spread
it into thin walls, spit casings for a whole
ochre nest to spin in their sleep.

       How did he first think to copy
these wasps? And what of the hot welts
on the tips of his fingers, and a whole
bracelet of heat around his wrist?
Did the welts interfere with his calligraphy,
each inky curl glowing black on flat silk
and brushed fatter than usual? Crispy bodies
collect near his candle, a light pile of wing
and mandible rolled into striped
commas, and still—he writes.

         I wonder about the space
between his legs, the void of tailed cells,
his skin there so alive with stringy nerve
but hardly touched. No chance for it to grow
resistant to a brush of the tiniest hand,
the coolness of a jade ring. His skin
there thin as the very paper
he first dried and cut clean.

Scott Owens

In the Cathedral of Fallen Trees

Each time he thinks something special
will happen, he'll see the sky resting
on bent backs of trees, he'll find
the wind hiding in hands of leaves,

he'll read some secret love scratched
in the skin of a tree just fallen.
Because he found that trees were not
forever, that even trees he knew

grew recklessly towards falling,
he gave in to wisteria's plan
to glorify the dead. He sat down
beneath the arches of limbs reaching

over him, felt the light spread
through stained glass windows of leaves,
saw every stump as a silent altar,
each branch a pulpit's tongue.

He did not expect the hawk to be here.
He had no design to find the meaning
of wild ginger, to see leaves soaked
with slime trails of things just past.

He thought only to listen
to the persistent breathing of trees,
to quiet whispers of leaves in wind,
secrets written in storied rings.

Each time he thinks something special
will happen. He returns with a handful
of dirt, a stone shaped like a bowl,
a small tree growing rootbound against a larger.

Scott Owens

Looking for Faces in the Night Sky

These are things anyone could have made
up. The stars are nothing but stars,
and playing dot-to-dot in the night
sky makes anything possible.
Years ago from the stone porch
my grandfather pointed them out:
the lion, the great bear, the hunter's sword.
This one he called Mary and showed me
how the stars made a woman's face.

Looking for faces in the night sky
we string stars into shapes of things
we fear or long to remember.
I see spider, sparrowhawk, bobwhite.
This one I'll call woman becoming
an angel, the grotesque buds of wings
sprouting in her back.

Scott Owens

Saint Sebastian's Widow

> *"A pious widow found him and nursed him back to health"* —
> Lives of the Saints

I found you, pierced with arrows and left
for dead, hanging by your hands
from a knotted oak, your head pitched
forward, face hidden beneath
the wet rag of your hair. I was old,

had been alone too long, had forgotten
how beautiful a man's chest could be,
the soft thatch of hair, small-boned
ribs pressing against the flesh,
curving around the heart. Even as you

were stretched to snapping, streaked with blood,
I wanted to cup my hands around
your breasts' unopened buds, lay my head
in the pale hollow of your chest,
rise and fall with your breathing.

I cut you down, broke off the arrows,
and struggled to carry you home,
not caring who saw me, what names
they called me. Once there I laid you
in my only bed, dug out the heads,

slowly, like pulling weeds, careful
to displace as little flesh as necessary,
sponging up blood and packing
wounds with my softest cloth.
For days your eyes stayed closed,

head lolling to one side, chest
barely moving. I dripped water

and broth slowly into your mouth.
I offered your body flowers and perfumes,
washed it daily with the best soaps

I could find, lingering over your soft
skin, the limp stem of your loins,
gently fingering each pale curve
of muscle, each ridge of bone.
At night when you moaned with pain,

I rushed to your side, watched your back
swell with air, held your face in my hands,
ran my fingers through your hair.
I wanted to lick the sweat from your brow,
suck the chill from your spine.

I nursed you back to consciousness,
kept you through your weakness,
fed you soup and bones and whatever
meat I could find, and you saying
nothing anyday but "Bless you."

When you started caring for yourself
again, I helped however I could,
enjoying the weight of your body on mine,
your arm thrown across my shoulders.
I knew you'd never stay.

On the first day you left the house,
you walked back to where I found you
and started preaching again.
A crowd gathered, first the people,
then the soldiers. I watched you

from below, only one of many.

Your face filled with glory,
eyes burning with conviction,
chest swelling beneath the robe
I'd made you. I barely understood

your words, but the soldiers knew you,
taunted you, spat at you,
called you ghost, deadman, Christian.
When you turned and swore at them,
condemned them, I saw the anger rise

in their faces. I saw them moving towards you.
I saw how you continued shouting
words like God, resurrection, salvation.
I wanted to stop you, to carry you home,
tell them it was only sickness speaking.

I did nothing. I watched them beat you
with clubs until your body was broken,
face bloated with bruises, chest
spattered with blood. I watched them
and cried to see your head give way.

I left you there for someone else
to bury, to chase the rats away,
clean your body, throw dirt across
what I had made so white.
I couldn't save you again. I left

as much alone as I had ever been.
I couldn't undo such ruin,
couldn't cry in your dead hair.
You, your own Sisyphus.
would never be my stone.

Scott Owens

Common Ground

My brother has never kept a single lake,
a single lost grave to himself.
Always he calls, then waits until I
can come, lets me lead the way,
find it like the first time,
shouting the names I know, the shapes
of bird and stone, cloud and tree.

Once in the same day I saw
a kestrel, a mantis, an arrowhead
and took it as a sign, though since
I have seen each in their own days
and miles away from each other.

I do not believe God will bend
to kiss this mouth. I do not believe
the wine will turn to blood. But something
knows the moment of sunflower,
the time of crow's open wing,
the span of moss growing on rock,
and water washing it away.

In the pictures I remember, there is you
letting me stand on the fallen tree
as if it were mine. There is you
letting my arm rest on top of yours
around our mother. There is you
lifting me up to the limb I couldn't reach.

This is the faith I've wanted, to know
that even now we are capable of such
sacrifice, such willingness to love.

Extremities

You can lose body parts
crossing a city street

you can lose your hands
inside the outstretched arms
of a woman's cardboard sign
disappear inside another country

you can lose your feet
inside the tap dancer's shoes,
the click, click, click on the pavement
a way to measure the world
as it falls away
in incremental eight counts

you can lose your skin to the wind
it finds the exact place where
your pores are most open
you can lose your organs
as they carefully fall outside of you
while you step into a cross walk

you can lose your brain as the pigeons
fly over you
as the taxi cab runs too close to the curb
and never understand why you were built
like this
barely sustainable
commanded to stay whole
while stepping over
your swollen self

as if all those pieces you've
picked up along the way
were never you

Linda Pastan

Encore
for RF

Before you go,
I would like to reprise for you
the blue cloud in the song's first stanza

and my own tears halfway down the page
which mark the score in half notes
or footprints in the disappearing distance.

I can still hear the applause—that winter thunder,
but let's forget the audience
some of whom are heading for the doors.

Let the violins be silent, their bows
like so many lopped branches
on the tree outside your frosted window.

Let all the fingers sleep
on the polished keys of all the pianos.
Let only percussions be left—

a cymbal like the bronze sun setting;
a drum beating time
to the fading pulse in your neck.

Linda Pastan

Beethoven's Quartet in C Major, Opus 59

The violins
are passionately
occupied, but
it is the cellist

who seems to be
holding the music
in his arms,
moving his bow

as if it were
a dowsing rod
and the audience
dying of thirst.

Linda Pastan

Why Are Your Poems So Dark?

Isn't the moon dark too,
most of the time?

And doesn't the white page
seem unfinished

without the dark stain
of alphabets?

When God demanded light,
he didn't banish darkness.

Instead he invented
ebony and crows

and that small mole
on your left cheekbone.

Or did you mean to ask
"Why are you sad so often?"

Ask the moon.
Ask what it has witnessed.

Linda Pastan

The Blackbirds

I can only call it post
post modern—this music

let loose by the blackbirds
as they swarm south

abandoning trees—
those leafy songbooks—

like individual notes
gone mad.

And the woods ring
with the first sounds

of autumn, raucous
and dark,

before a single
leaf has changed.

Linda Pastan

Shoe

A world without you—surreal
as a painting I studied once
of a fur-lined teacup.

But what to make of a shoe
filled with tears,
or a signpost pointing

backwards, or faces
featureless as moons? Dreams
lie, as promises do.

I rest half in, half out of sleep,
the morning light a knife
at the window sill.

Linda Pastan

Cassandra

There are so few of them
at first
a mere rustle

on the wind
with just a hint of red
or gilt along their edges,

and the mother woods
are still green,
and the sun still spills

its molten light
on upturned faces;
no one worries

if a few are falling—
they are simply
grace notes,

wisps of portent,
though soon they turn
acrobatic

showing their bellies
to the breeze,
soon a few more

wordlessly
shake loose—early soldiers
of the season,

no smoke yet,
no raging flames
of color.

But make no mistake,
something is coming
to an end.

Doug Ramspeck

Fox Lake

Maybe they are lovers—
        or maybe they are carved
in rock at twilight.

But if the lake is smeared
        gray and sensual
beyond the cattails,

here is the impulse permanently transfixed,
        the pale, placid faces
revealing nothing,

like lost bodies floating toward you in a dream,
        held aloft
in a statue's fragmentation—

or as iridescent flesh transformed
        to moonlight,
like what's shaped

and then discarded in the stone.

Doug Ramspeck

After That

In the mornings now she walks
into the slash pines. She used to walk
all the way to the river, but now she stops
by the railroad tracks. Ghosts are gathered
amid the blackjack oaks, but that is not
why she won't go farther. She used to be happy
enough to feel the ghosts trying to reform
their bodies in the wedge-shaped leaves.
It pleased her to sense them crowding in,
as though to press close was a kind
of remembering, though she could not
herself imagine wanting to remember living
through someone else's body. Her husband
once told her he thought often
of the skeleton inside him, picturing
the scaffolding of bones and its temporary
flesh, as though our true selves did not exist
until we were stripped finally of the mask.
In the summer of the drought she walked
with him one morning to see how the river
had dried and congealed to mud and rocks.
Even then you could tell that something was alive.
You could see where the water had carved
its name into the banks, where the exposed
roots of the trees had been washed and battered.
For a moment she had held his hand,
but all she could think about were the bones
beneath his skin, the bones beneath her skin,
and the water that had vanished without rain.

Mary Kay Rummel

Firebird

You fly around the volcano,
a dragonfly near a fire,
you forget your own hills...

The Seine threads quicksilver.
Peonies droop—exhausted ballerinas.
Trees brood in green cassocks,
shift toward solstice
through smoke, no incense.

Even at Monet's Giverny
under the citron blooms,
tunnels hazed with cigarettes,
the smell of life-used-up.

Hawks circle the garden,
angry when they snag a tourist
hidden beneath wisteria
on the Japanese bridge.

Still, this city murmurs
inside paintings, inside songs
that line your hands.

Paris mutates beneath your touch.
Gothic seethes underneath rococo,
portraits fly apart under concrete.

Energy giving, energy taking—
peony pirouettes in a crypt.
Burning beneath rose windows,
flying buttresses, your light hypotenuse.

All your changes among the fires,
flicker in the eye of a gargoyle.

Wounded Angel

Too many spires—
more bells than she had feathers.

Warm-hearted sins wearing crimson dresses
in blazing gardens waved her in.

She shed radiance—the look of grace
a folded white robe at her breast.

Standing there nude and alone as rain
as many sleepless eyes on her body
as once were feathers—she thought on his desire.

Like the bleating wave tracing the line of foam
she wanted to touch those fringes
of soul on his surface.

Everything moving up from trees
allowed direct speaking from the wound.

She heard a roar of wings, a deeper flesh—
running through acres of time and wheat

until she fell, her beehive body
sheltering one holy thing

a red-tipped feather from her unfinished
leave-taking wings.

C. J. Sage

The Weatherman's Broken Promise

It did not flurry at the beach and that's okay—I talked someone into sending me a snowball. I was older when it arrived and I'd forgotten the head I'd planned it for, so I collared a new victim in calf-skin gloves. I do not kneel in church because I do not go to church—my mouth carries that charge although sometimes it slips up, cracking vaults and scrambling the codes of innocents. If cars are the body in dreams, then maybe radios are breath. Maybe gasps. Escher's stairs and fields without set paths: if I flew, those would be the destinations. Let's jet: you be weightless now and I'll be dust.

C. J. Sage

Sonnet for Carryhouse and Keeper

I met a man who'd kept a snail as a pet
beneath a cold stone house which held no wife
(too dank for even long-stray cats to thrive).
Inside an old fish tank his snail friend slept.

The man's round back was proof he'd not forget
to spend good time just keeping things alive
between his care-filled self and his shelled bride.
All day he'd curve around her as she crept

among the leafy shadows of his hands;
he'd trace her pearl-string trails with his fingers,
his breath would set small clouds into her glass.

The day he set her free she took one half
the day to slip into good-bye; she lingered
in the lovegrass, like the lovelorn, said this man.

C. J. Sage

Open House

I'm not giving up
my hand-over-heart casting,
my moonlight-roofed hatch

to the stars' bridle.
Others are left to rot;
I pick up the kicked-down

ladder. I only want to hoist your
private holdings: look over there.
To that soft spot in everyone

I tender rolls: the slender,
sand-filled shoulders
of a road. I couldn't wield a rake

if a bank account depended on it,
but I'll tongue your bar graphs
high into your sternums.

I'll jungle gym your rafters
to show where the sun rises.
Snuff is not in my vocabulary,

so I'll stand with a light bulb chain,
pulling and pulling.
There are no better explanations

than a platinum-haired creature
working her wrists.
I am here in the haystack

of your curbsides,
glinting like a sharp
until you find me.

Rebecca Seiferle

Two Versions of Bear Canyon

I.
standing beside her, as she sits on a rock beneath
the quietest of skies, the stars paused like the punctum

in night's wrist, my hand touches her shoulder, my thumb
traces the edges of bone beneath her pale and velvet—there

where her skin is naked to the air, as we both somehow are
naked here, cleansed, as if bathed in the living water that pours

without measure from the black stone of the mountain, the body
so present, along the southward horizon, the palpable form

of the earth dreaming—wondering how she can feel the feeling
in me, if it flows like water through fingertips and cells, as something,

whatever it is. . . inexhaustible. . . flows around and within
and out of the space in which we stand, so two

most human animals, beneath these clouds whose light
feathers the dark space behind them, so

in inexhaustible love, this space, so empty, is devoid
of nothing. It holds within its untiring hand, the constellated

pinpoints of light, the clouds with their plumes of breath,
the stretch of the road toward the southward horizon, where a sign

marks the end of the road for any travel other than travel
that goes on by foot, and the mountains themselves, whose body

in my gaze is soft, malleable, a kind of visual embrace, as if
I were held in the arms of the earth, as I hold her in the arms

of the embrace of my breath and my being, and does
it flow through the air, around and within, this boundariless

feeling, and does she feel how it wells up in me, so full of
the darkest, sweetest, most living, water, how the deepest

layers in me have opened like the rock shivering along
its mineral vein, to open into this space, ever flowering

night of my desire for her, where I so feel the feeling in me
that it's the body of the mountains and the sky and stars

and even the few stars of the Great Bear that has dipped
behind the sharp edge of a peak, so present

this love for her, it wells up in me
and fills up my lip, like the bite of a kiss, an anointing

of some more living coal of desire, as if she were a world
that she holds me within, a space so orchard

it is devoid of nothing, quiet as the pulse in her delirious wrist.

2.
When the road ends, I am standing beside
her, as she shadows a rock
beneath the sky where a bear pulses the dark with starfire,

those seven stars scooping out the darkness

in ancient night's wrist:
my hand touches her shoulder, my thumb
traces the edges of bone beneath her pale and velvet; there,

on the shoulder of the bear, a cup, or the farrowing of the plough;

her skin is naked to the air, as we both somehow are naked here,
divesting ourselves of our private stories,
the flayed skin of our myths.

> *how Callisto, a servant of Artemis,*
> *lay down with Zeus when he tricked her, appearing in the form of Artemis.*

Along the southward horizon, the palpable form
of dreaming and wonder flows through fingertips and cells,

> *So she lay down,*

as something, whatever it is, so gardened and honeyed, flows
around and within the space in which we breathe, so two

> *she thought,*

most naked animals, beneath these clouds whose light
feathers the dark—limitless and ever pouring forth—

> *the Earth was young,*

so devoid of nothing, it holds
in its inexhaustible hand:

> *playing the bear*

the constellated
pinpoints of light, the clouds, the plumes of our breath,

> *with a goddess. She thought*

the stretch of the road toward the south horizon, the sign
that marks the end of any travel other than travel that goes on by foot,

> *the wind was singing*

the mountains themselves, as if the deepest geological layers
of the body had opened, the black rock, slivering

and threw them into the sky:

its mineraled vein, to pour forth its dark sweet water.
Animals move through the body of the mountains and the sky,

the asterism, and there it lay shattered—

and the constellations are shedding their stories
like two undressing to their bright skins.

the recognizable form of the less discernible—

How the present wells up
and fills my lip, like the bite of a kiss: this world

who almost slew her with an arrow,

we hold each other within, oh space so orcharded
it is devoid of nothing, alive as the pulse in my delirious wrist.

until she heard the wind singing:

When the earth holds us, it holds us like this.

Rebecca Seiferle

A Broken Crown of Sonnets for My Father's Forehead

7.

Not in the kingdom of death, in the jar
of my childhood, a male seahorse floated
like debris. Solo, thickening, in a tear
of Morton salt and tap water, he snorkeled
up pink clouds of shrimp, and gave birth to four
children, each a tiny Pegasus, whirring
through a bare and gelid world, circling
his great hippocampus head. Who was I
to fathom such a creature, concoct a sea
within a jar? When I lifted the glass,
the tide of my touch sent him crashing. He
could only drift in the directionless ache,
as his young vanished, one by one, his pouch
filled with nothing but the current itself.

Rebecca Seiferle

The Foundling

The only ghost I've ever seen
was that of a baby black bear, waiting

for me one night in the kitchen in Salmon, Idaho,
a small green tornado caught in the corner by the stove,

full of pale yellow lights like the tiny polished stones
that flash in the bed of the coldest mountain streams.

All winter, we lived in that rented house, while the landlord,
in the garage, practiced his butcher's art, skinning, gutting, disassembling

whatever the local hunters brought him—and I'd seen the cub
hanging outside my window. Flayed of its rich black skin,

reduced to the scaffold of its bones, its overlay of red muscle and white fat,
without claws or snout, pud or tail of bear, it hung in the glare

of the porch light like a human child. So when I went roaming
the silenced house so late at night and was met by that wild presence,

I spoke to it until it sighed and vanished into the peeling wall,
and left me, the only child still there, snared in the net of the world.

Rebecca Seiferle

Bat in a Jar

The jar was a mason jar, made to preserve
apricots and stone cherries and to withstand
the extremes of cold air and hot water baths
where the steam, rising, lifts
the canner's black lid
only to drop it, hissing, again. And the bat,
trapped inside knew, if it knew anything,
it would never escape, though
the sky kept humming
with insects and the orchards darkened
as usual, *apparently* the same.

Someone had put the bat in a jar—to avoid
bites and disease or to protect
the bat itself from house cats and dogs?
In any case, the bat kept calling
for rescue, measuring what confined it, trying
to scale the horizon, that sky of glass. But though
the bat's ears shaped themselves
to the echo, though the echo
filled the glass, the jar parodied
the bat's longing and gave back
nothing of itself.

Mirrored, only the bat was mirrored. Its fear
inaudible except to itself, confined
to its own mind. That which enabled
the bat to select a mosquito
or to nip a June beetle out of the air
now sickened it. Open-mouthed,
wings beating hopefully, hopelessly, the bat
lifted its wing like one seamless membrane
and again and again
tried to answer.

John Siddique

Fragment

Words suddenly light in the mind,
love is like death, it can come at any moment.
It is never expected, and nothing is the same again.
All that came before it—all that follows after
—is nothing but time.

Love is like life; we are bracketed by time,
so much silence surrounding us, uncountable
words suddenly in the mind.

I knew you must exist, how could you not
when I had dreamed, thought and spoken
the possibility of you all my life.

Many women came disguised as you,
sent as a test. I am no good at tests.
I forgot your name and life.
I became cheap.
I dressed well—beautifully.
The heart without love.

Love is like death,
it arrives at any moment unbidden.
Grown from seeds of forever,
we have the taste of it in our mouths all our lives.
A savour running through all things.

Love is like life, surrounded by silence.
—Half words trying to resolve into being.

John Siddique

Adultery

Finally I reached across the table
to touch your face, the pads of my fingers
on your forehead first, drawing down near
the inner edge of your ear and under
to hold your chin, lifting your head slightly
as if I'm about to kiss you.

We are burning as if we are adulterers.
The table is between us to keep us apart.
I think if we are going to have to pay for this,
I want to have at least touched your skin.
We do not kiss, don't go home, or make love,
we drink tea—green for you, regular black tea
for me. I eat, you say you can't.

We are adulterers of talk and desire,
pretending that by not coming together
we are somehow still standing on the good side
of the line.

We sit amongst other lovers, no one knows
we are not supposed to be, say my name, you say,
and I say it. I want to show you so many things,
you say. It goes right into the place
I have covered up and armoured, to pretend
it no longer existed.

Jeffrey Side

Plaster Piece

The sky-blue plaster piece
you chose because I touched it,
you will always keep.
You like to spend the days with me.

The Sunday I first took you
on plastic with red button lens
you turned out well.
The air was cold, but it was shining.

And the round crowned church
held you in its circle
and calmed you at my side.

You take photos in the light.

Judith Skillman

The Water Lily

Residue of a past
layered deeply over time present.
Burnt Norton come to water.

Ritual gestures of a sun
too pale to care or cure.
Edge looped over edge,
the pine cone sustains rodents.

The dirt is deeper than we are
and more humble. Doesn't mind
a vine or two
crumpled across its face.

Bitten like a fruit, no longer meant
to name the animals
or count rotten obsessions
of a language

too dark to matter.
This lily is not bloody.
It floats on a ceiling of water,
braided tendrils unencumbered
by false modesty.

If this was the place where Mallarme
first passed the entrance
of the page, then beyond would be
an island inhabited
by Rousseau's sleepy plants.

Craig Colin Smith

Song of Oak

Now. The movement fades and finishes.
The wind holds its breath with us.
No vibrato of bark,
no tremolo of leaf,
no quaver of twig,
Fall falls silent.
Now. The movement begins.
Huddled at the knees of our oak
with our ears cupped to the drumhead
of the earth, we listen for the undertones
growing, rising from the low, slow, pounding root.

Craig Colin Smith

Tides

Call moon, call water, call love.
Essential has a simple, not single, name
and forever needs another:
form mouth, form hands to form the things
that form the time to come.
If moon: try crescents and wax and wane
the phases of lunacy and tides.
If water: try swallows and tears and falls
the increase of erosion and tides.
If love: try moonlight and seas and lost
the never of forever and tides.
Essential has a single, not simple, name
and never needs no other:
form mouth, form hands to form the things
that form the time to go.
Call love, call water, call moon.

J.R. Solonche

Elegy For A House Finch Killed Against The Window Glass

If words can be a grave,
then let these be yours.
I will try to make them
at least as soft as the fresh
dead leaves fallen onto
the bed of myrtle, the place
where I have placed you
to pass the winter. Let all
be soft now. We are both
to blame, I more so than
you. Let me speak softly.
So much of the world is
so hard. At times, too much.
If words can be soft,
let them be these. Or if these
be too hard, let two be soft
enough for you, or one,
just one, like leaves.

Joannie Stangeland

August Is Just Long

Summer stains green, a tarnish.
The maples' thick leaves shut
out the sun, an airless shade.
Some respite.

So many voices
couch the quiet, the season
swelling even as it dies.

One rosebud unfolds,
an older bloom withered, spent.

Your purse is empty.

Night comes sooner. And yet,
warmth on your arms,
a jay in the birch, a rhythm
to the rustling.

The smallest pock of trust.

Oh blue for the sky—yes,
it's a wide-open prayer.

Red for the door,
your heart you open.

Tim Suermondt

City For The Taking

From the rooftop restaurant
the woman surveys the great city,
smaller but greater now
given her point of view:
"I was always a little afraid
of the city when I was a child," she says,
"but look, I can reach out
and pick up these tall buildings
like they were toys."
The man who's been preoccupied
with his Mexican chili sauce
says, "All you know about life
is what you know about life."
It's a joke, yet an explanation.
The woman brings a hand
lightly to her throat and laughs—
a red ribbon scuds through
the air, effortlessly.

Maria Terrone

Introducing the Forest to Vivaldi

Ignore the crows, their rude calls from the balcony
of trees. This concert piped through speakers
isn't meant for them but you: dulcet chorus of vireos,
cardinals, wrens, doves, whose daily rhapsody
goes unapplauded. Allow yourselves a brief
intermission and settle into plush evergreen.
Listen to the strings and flutes, how they seem
to imitate you in their fluttering grief
and patient beseeching. But how can
we match a music of constant hunger and quick
relief, your allegro heartbeat, life a short, lit wick?
If this serenade can offer any lesson,
it will after the last note, when silence swells
your throats with its hum and seeps
into folded wings like the moment before sleep.

Maria Terrone

Words to Unpin Yourself From the Wall

You want to be somewhere else, out of
the three-hour lecture, the marathon reading,
out of your pinned skin, inside
the wild commotion of small birds hidden
within a massive tree that seems to swell and vibrate.
To be inside one feathered throat pulsing and the vortex
of autumn leaves pulling the last light to itself.
Tell them you must go, then speak no more. Risk all
for the last leaf and the other-wordly calls at liftoff.
Feel the magnetic imperative of that high,
black string drawn across continents. Stay
until you can't see sky or the upturned face
of the stranger who's joined you,
and it's the wind that has the last word,
blowing sharp leaves at your lips—
such rough, red kisses.

Maria Terrone

Artist "Anon"

1. Embroiderer of the Emperor's Robes
Summoned as a boy, he stays alive
in the Forbidden City by weaving
memories with the silk of his mother's hair,
green thread of mountain mornings.
I squint before its dazzle,
searching for the old, conscripted tailor.
He hides, a bent shadow
on the retinue's fringe, spent eyes
narrowing to the eye of his needle.

2. Etcher of Scrimshaw
Exiled sailor,
a fallen-down drunk lassoed
by deck rope, tossed by anger's maelstrom.
But when sunk in loneliness,
he conjures wife and son
on bone: amazing,
how the homesick heart
can guide the improbable hand
to this precise and spidery black art.

3. Itinerant Painter
He travels the Roman Empire by cart
and foot, grinding purple seashells,
gathering soil, soot, and chalk, crushing
colored stones. The names of senators,
centurions and prosperous olive merchants
are lost in time. Yet century after century
his subjects gaze with all-knowing eyes,
familiar to each generation. The faceless
painter? Returned to his element,
he can be found everywhere:
in shell, soil, soot, chalk, stone.

4. Immigrant Seamstress

And what of the girl whom steerage
nearly tore to tatters?
All the doors are locked and exits blocked
in her new country of sorrow.
Even in waning light, she bends
to stitch ten thousand jet beads
onto this black opera cloak
for a patron of the arts
whose name we still revere.
Unfurled on the scarred workbench,
it reminds her of the starlings—
the way hundreds, flashing iridescence,
would sweep down, then settle,
on the rocky fields back home.

Maria Terrone

The Egyptian Queen Gives Death the Slip

Found: two boxes of wigs in my tomb
and a stash of makeup; considering my rain-
soaked sail to the other side, you assume
a queen needs to freshen up. But no, I changed
looks to slip by unknown in last century's hairstyle
and dated powder shades like bronze and clay.
You've seen my "death mask" in the museum's Nile
wing by an artist I hired myself. Pray,
do I look dumb or weak? When you stared
into my black-winged eyes, weren't you first to blink?
Taking flight is my talent. Let Death play solitaire,
or else play with you his eternal, stinking
game of boredom. That's not for me. I'm everywhere
and nowhere, which is why you found my casket bare.

Maria Terrone

A Poet in the Customs House

Pleased by my jottings, the President
found me employment. Now
I work on a civil temple on a tongue
of land that speaks the Babel
of ivory tusks, bolts of silk, cinnamon
and jasmine tea, each item to be weighed,
counted, and assessed in the definitive language
of ledgers, my eye trained to detect,
then reject, what's tainted,
too dangerous to wave through.
While merchants line up to pay,
my mind wanders across its Bosporus
of time. Today, a lamb's wool shawl
trussed me in childhood till the sweat
began to pour: yesterday, a crystal vial released
a musky night I thought I'd stoppered.
On breaks, I need to gaze on the black,
opaque sea, breathing deeply.
But then another ship appears,
bearing poems I can't appraise
among its dense, resplendent cargo.

K.J. Van Deusen

This Wind

> *A leaf trembles. I tremble*
> *in the wind-beauty like silk from Turkestan.*
> *The censer fans into flame.*
> *This wind is the Holy Spirit.*
>   —Rumi

There's something thrilling and glassy in the air -
like Celtic harp playing or hammered dulcimer -
something shining the unmown grass,
shining the leaves,
polishing the gold and silver ornaments
on the Christmas garland we left up over the porch
all winter and all spring.

Up in the corner, an arm's reach away
the house finch hatchlings,
perfect and newly-feathered,
present themselves, lean out
their nest of birch twigs and artificial pine.
Their gleaming black eyes,
small as seeds, wide as the world,
look past me to the white birch
where their mother and father
are swinging on thin branches
that arch down like willow,
swinging sun to shade
in a canopy of light
as green as the first morning of creation.

The hatchlings yearn, they hesitate.
And the mother and the father
keep calling to them,
"Come! Come into this wind!"

Black Skies

The sun bottoms out
and they rise again,

air-tumbling whorls,
screaming four-letter words.

When our backs are turned
they go straight for the warm blood,

dying their beaks
in our carbon dioxide,

clicking their beaks
like mad scissors.

Joseph says their magic is in the feathers,
he calls them quills that ink the skies.

I say, strange they bleed cold.
But, Ah—respite,

he with the bow and arrow,
he with the eyes

in the back of his head,
he with the illusion of time.

Marc Vincenz

Crushed Dragon Bones
Tiger Claw Apothecary, Shanghai, 1999

Quan leads me through an array of popping scents,
this lingering whiff of Bombay spice bazaar,

medicine healing scars, prehensile fungi, blooming
rhino horn, white deer antler, mandible of stag beetle,

snapping tail of scorpion, turtle snout, all crushed to steep
in clear hot liquids bubbling right into the very centre

of the maze where a woman in a nightdress waits patiently.
Here he goes whispering in the corner.

Lady behind the counter turns flushed-cheek red,
titters under her breath, holds her hand to cover her teeth.

Eyes him apprehensively. Eyebrows arch-raised,
coughs in syncopated answer. Fiddles with her stethoscope.

Another woman looks me up and down: Hey you, big nose?
Want me check your pulse? I sit down across the counter.

She applies the leather-puffing contraption to my left bicep.
Pumps until I feel my left side is ready to explode.

Aha, take this. She fiddles a powder, rattling grains from
that drawer, granules from another. All marked in red.

Grinds the mixture in mortar humming some old love tune.
Flips the dust into a paper bag. Hand palm out:

Fifty yuan. Releases the catch and Ssssss spins down.
Quan's smiling ear to ear and we're out the door

through the hedgerows and into haze of open space.
Quan rumbles something about bones old bones.

Crushed dragon bones for the little man inside.
No problem like you, he says. This will keep me going all
night.

Jane Yolen

Color Poem for a Painter Friend

Of all the colors of your life,
these are the wisest:
ultramarine of sea
slapping against the rocks,
sap green sliding down
the bark of a tree,
the deep terre verte
of rooted things,
sienna fingerlets on twig ends,
the cadmium red rush
of time spilling out
from a finger pricked by a rose.

Jane Yolen

The Making of Poetry

"How it bevels common glass..."
—Tom Ayers

Shadows in the grass,
Moss inscription on rock,
Reflection in the beveled glass,
A short, sharp aftershock.

All the poetry in the world
Cannot bring you back.

Jane Yolen

Bird Recordist

What a strange bird the recordist is.
Up at dawn, check.
Listens to the chorus. Check.
Takes out his parabolic mike.
Waits a minute.
Presses record.
Captures song.
Brings it home.
And then bird song fills the room:
    The jubilant invitations to a nest;
    Harsh challenges to a rival;
    Sweet, soaring seductions;
    Bold warnings to a fox or raptor or passing owl;
    Praise of succulent berries;
    And the querulous rantings of the unwanted male.

The recordist never opens his own mouth,
But his ears—oh his ears—are ready, content full,
A blevit of sound.

Tomorrow he will find another glen.

Desmond Kon Zhicheng-Mingdé

a faded postcard is a tanka daydream

but of the firewalker
of his frame, a rush of flame

look at both faces, closed eyes

this, what you were born into
to grasp, that expectation
a forward hesitation—

to love only once
to endure, outlast these worlds
a lowing, literal love

not the bitter deathsong ends
not the judging eyes

a milk bath before
fresh plate of malai kofta

look at the firewalker—

dusted feet and flake, embers
as windblown, the water oak
next to the winged spindle tree

Publication Credits

Kim Addonizio
"For You" and "Lucifer at the Starlite" from *Lucifer at the Starlite* by Kim Addonizio, (W.W. Norton & Company, Inc. 2009). Used by permission of author.

Malaika King Albrecht
"Beyond the Clover Meadow" and "The Secret Keeper" appear in *What the Trapeze Artist Trusts* (Press 53, 2012).

Kimberly L. Becker
"This morning found" by Kimberly L. Becker, published in *Words Facing East*, (WordTech Editions, Cincinnati, Ohio, 2011). Reprinted by permission.

Michelle Bitting
"Sacrament" first appeared in *The Southeast Review* and is from *Good Friday Kiss* (C & R Press, 2008)
"The Sacrifice" first appeared in Rattle and is from Good Friday Kiss (C & R Press, 2008)

Karen Bowles
"Receding" (*Luciole Press*, Winter 2008).

David Caddy
"Wild Swans At Stur Mill" appears in *The Bunny Poems* (Shearsman Books, 2011).

Beth Copeland
"Thumbnail Moon" and "Similitude" appear in *Transcendental Telemarketer*, (BlazeVOX Books, 2012).

Alison Croggon
"Divinations" and "Intimations" from *The Common Flesh* (Arc Publications, 2003).
"Moon" and "All Souls Day" from *Theatre* (Salt Publishing, 2008)

Rachel Dacus
"Chopin Reigns" appears in *Gods of Water and Air* (Aldrich Press, 2013)

J.P. Dancing Bear
"Blue Mountain at Sunset" from *The Abandoned Eye* (FutureCycle Press, 2012).
"The Magician's Assistant", "Night as a Love Poem", and "Dia de los Muertos" from *Inner Cities of Gulls* (SalmonPoetry, 2010).

Lori Desrosiers
"Les Cigales" from *New Millenium Review 2012* (finalist), and in *The Philosopher's Daughter* (Salmon Poetry 2013).

Brian Fone
"Black Cockatoos" appears in *Selected Poems* by Brian Fone (Lulu, 2011).

Amy George
"Zen Garden" appears in *The Fragrance of Memory* (Amsterdam Press, 2009).

David M. Harris
"Nightfall" appears in *The Review Mirror* (Unsolicited Press, 2013).

Mary Hutchins Harris
"Kyrie" and "King Solomon's Overture" were published in *A Tongue Full of Yeses* (Stepping Stones Press, 2008).

Jane Hirshfield
"When Your Life Looks Back" first appeared in *American Poetry Review*, September/October 2009 issue: Vol.38/No.5 and in *Come Thief* (Knopf, 2011).
"Not Moving Even One Step" from *The Lives of the Heart* (HarperCollins, 1997).
"In a Net of Blue and Gold" from *Of Gravity & Angels* (Wesleyan University Press, 1988).
"Pyracantha and Plum" from *After* (HarperCollins Publishers, 2006).
"Leaving the October Palace" from *The October Palace* (HarperCollins, 1994).

Robert S. King
"The Landowners of Pompeii", first published in *Pirene's Fountain*, appears in *One Man's Profit* (Sweatshoppe Publications, 2013).

Rustin Larson
"The Emperor's Tapestry" from *Calliope*.
"Notebook" from *Baybury Review*.
Both poems appear in *The Wine-Dark House* (Blue Light Press, 2009).
"The Collected Discography of Morning" and "Life Documented" first appeared in *Pirene's Fountain*. Both poems appear in *Bum Cantos, Winter Jazz, & The Collected Discography of Morning*, winner of the 2013 Blue Light Book Award (Blue Light Press, San Francisco).

Dorianne Laux
"Trees are Time" first published in *Pirene's Fountain*, October 2008.
"Cello" from *Facts About the Moon* (W.W. Norton & Company, Inc., 2007).
"Heart" from: *Smoke* (BOA Editions, Ltd., 2000).
"The Shipfitter's Wife" from: *Smoke* (BOA Editions, Ltd., 2000).

Aine MacAodha
"Mise Eire" first published in *The Argotist Online*.

Catherine McGuire
"Wild Carrot" appears in *Glimpses of a Garden* (Lulu, 2012).

Amy MacLennan
"I Close My Eyes When I Listen to Poetry" from *The Sand Hill Review*, 2005.

Joseph Millar
"Love Pirates" from *Overtime* (Eastern Washington University Press, 2001).
"Coming Home" from *Fortune* (Eastern Washington University Press, 2007).
"Poem for Rembrandt" from *Fortune* (Eastern Washington University Press, 2007).

Jim Moore
"Two Flute Songs" from *THE NEW BODY* (University of Pittsburgh, 1976).

Lisel Mueller
"Stalking the Poem" from *Alive Together*, LSU Press. Copyright © Lisel Mueller. Printed by permission of the publisher.

Aimee Nezhukumatathil
"The Latch" and "The Light I Collect" first published in *Pirene's Fountain*, appears in *LUCKY FISH* (Tupelo Press, 2011).

Scott Owens
"In the Cathedral of Fallen Trees," *Something Knows the Moment* (Main Street Rag, 2011).
"Looking for Faces in the Night Sky," *Something Knows the Moment* (Main Street Rag, 2011).
"St. Sebastian's Widow," *Something Knows the Moment* (Main Street Rag, 2011).
"Common Ground," *Something Knows the Moment* (Main Street Rag, 2011).

Linda Pastan
"Cassandra" first appeared in *The American Scholar*.
"Shoe" first appeared in *New Letters*.
"The Blackbirds" first appeared in *Prairie Schooner*.
"why are your poems so dark?", "Beethoven's Quartet in C Major, Opus 59", and "Encore," from *Queen of a Rainy Day* by Linda Pastan: Copyright © 2006 by Linda Pastan. Used by permission of W.W. Norton & Company, Inc.

Mary Kay Rummel
"Wounded Angel": Linsteadt, Stephen. *Woman in Metaphor* (An ArtPoetry book) in press.

C.J. Sage
"Sonnet for Carryhouse and Keeper" from *The San Simeon Zebras* (Salmon 2010).
"Open House" from *Open House* (Salmon 2014).

Rebecca Seiferle
"Two Versions of Bear Canyon" first published in *Pirene's Fountain* (May 2009).
"A Broken Crown of Sonnets for My Father's Forehead, # 7" from *The Music We Dance To* (Sheep Meadow Press, 1999).
"The Foundling" from *Bitters* (Copper Canyon Press, 2001).
"Bat in a Jar" from *The Ripped Out Seam* (Sheep Meadow Press, 1993).

John Siddique
"Adultery" appears in *Full Blood* (Salt Publishing 2011).

Maria Terrone
"Artist Anon" from *Atlanta Review, Vol. XI, No. 1, Fall/Winter 2004*.
"The Egyptian Queen Gives Death the Slip" from *The Hudson Review, Vol. LV, Number 2, Summer 2002*.
"A Poet in the Customs House" from *Atlanta Review, Vol. XII, No. 1, Fall/Winter 2005*.

K.J. Van Deusen
"This Wind" appears in the print anthology *Granite Island, Amber Sea: Writings from the Black Hills and Plains*.

Authors

Kim Addonizio's most recent poetry collection is *Lucifer at the Starlite* (W.W. Norton). A collection of stories, *The Palace of Illusions*, is forthcoming from Counterpoint/ Soft Skull. She lives in Oakland, CA and offers online workshops. Visit her at www.kimaddonizio.com.

Malaika King Albrecht is the author of three poetry books. Her most recent book *What the Trapeze Artist Trusts* is available at Press 53 and won honorable mention in the Oscar Arnold Young Award. Her chapbook *Lessons in Forgetting* was published by Main Street Rag and was a finalist in the 2011 Next Generation Indie Book Awards and received honorable mention in the Brockman Campbell Award. Her second book *Spill* was also published by Main Street Rag in 2011. Her poems have been published in many literary magazines and anthologies and nominated for Pushcarts. Her poems have won awards in several contests, including at *Poetry Southeast*, the North Carolina Poetry Council, Salem College and Press 53. She's the founding editor of *Redheaded Stepchild*, an online magazine that only accepts poems that have been rejected elsewhere. She lives in Ayden, N.C. with her family and is a therapeutic riding instructor.

Kimberly L. Becker is a member of Wordcraft Circle of Native Writers and Storytellers and author of two poetry collections from WordTech Editions, *Words Facing East* (2011) and *The Dividings* (forthcoming). Her poems appear widely in journals and anthologies, including the "Native American Women's Poetry" folio in *Drunken Boat* and *Women Write Resistance: Poets Resist Gender Violence* (Hyacinth Girl Press, 2013). Recipient of county and state grants (MD), she has also held residencies at Hambidge and Weymouth. Kimberly has been a featured reader at many venues, including "Native Writers in DC" at the Smithsonian's National Museum of the American Indian. Current projects include adapting traditional Cherokee stories into plays for the Cherokee Youth in Radio Project in Cherokee, NC. Visit her at www.kimberlylbecker.com

R. Steve Benson's book of poems "Schooled Lives: Poems By Two Brothers," co-authored with his brother, was published in 2009. The Christian Science Monitor has published 20 of his shorter poems and his poems have appeared in dozens of literary journals across America.

Michelle Bitting grew up near the Pacific Ocean and has work published or forthcoming in The American Poetry Review, Prairie Schooner, Narrative, River Styx, Crab Orchard Review, diode, Linebreak, the L.A. Weekly, and others. *Poems have appeared on Poetry Daily and as the Weekly Feature on Verse Daily. Thomas Lux chose her full-length manuscript, Good Friday Kiss,* as the winner of the DeNovo First Book Award and C & R Press published it in 2008. Her book *Notes to the Beloved* won the 2011 Sacramento Poetry Center Award and was published in 2012. Michelle has taught poetry in the U.C.L.A. Extension Writer's Program, at Twin Towers prison with a grant from Poets & Writers Magazine and is proud to be an active California Poet in the Schools. She holds an MFA in Poetry from Pacific University, Oregon and recently commenced work on a PhD in Mythological Studies at Pacifica Graduate Institute. She lives in Los Angeles with her husband, actor Phil Abrams and their two children. Visit her at www.michellebitting.com

Karen Bowles is the founder and publisher of Luciole Press (www.luciolepress.com), an international publication dedicated to all arts and cultures. She also works as an editor, advisor, writer, and reviewer. Contact her at karenbowles@luciolepress.com, and check out her page at www.facebook.com/BowlesKaren. She graduated from San Francisco State University with a B.A. in Literature; loves photography, reading, painting, and Sci-Fi movies. Her work has been published in *Pirene's Fountain's Sunrise from Blue Thunder*, multiple literary journals, reviews, on book covers, and will appear in many forthcoming publications. "Firefly," a nickname given to her by author/poet S.A. Griffin due to her enduring love of glowbugs, shines forth in the name of her press – "Luciole" is French for firefly. You can usually find her gazing at stars and arguing with bossy blue jays.

Cynthia Brackett-Vincent was nominated for the Pushcart Prize with her poem, "Come Morning" which appears in this anthology. She has published/edited *The Aurorean* poetry journal since 1995 and has had over 100 of her own poems plus nonfiction published in the United States and abroad. Her 2012 co-edited anthology, *Women on Poetry: Writing, Revising, Publishing and Teaching* (McFarland) was named one of 100 Best Books for Writers by *Poets & Writers*. Cynthia holds a BFA in Creative Writing from the University of Maine at Farmington and is pursuing her MA in English/Creative Writing—Poetry at Southern New Hampshire University to prepare to teach poetry writing at the community college level. She lives in Maine with her husband and their three rescue cats where she enjoys hiking and snowshoeing. She has three grown sons, three daughters-in-law, and five grandchildren. She considers, "Grammie, what does poetry mean?" (from six-year old Noah) to be one of the best questions she has ever been asked. Visit http://www.encirclepub.com

David Caddy is a poet, essayist, critic, literary sociologist and historian. He lives and works in rural Dorset from where he edits international literary journal *Tears in the Fence*. His most recent books include a literary travel novella, *Cycling After Thomas And The English* (Spout Hill Press 2013) and a collection of literary essays, *So Here We Are* (Shearsman Books 2012). His poetry books include *The Bunny Poems* (Shearsman 2011), *Man in Black* (Penned in the Margins 2007), and *The Willy Poems* (Clamp Down Press USA 2004). David is a long-standing promoter of poetry and co-author of London: City of Words (2006), a literary companion, with Westrow Cooper. He founded the East Street Poets in 1985, which he ran until 2001, and directed the Wessex Poetry Festival from 1995 until 2002. He subsequently organized the Tears in the Fence Festival 2003-2005. A new book of poems and literary travel book are in the pipeline.

Jessie Carty's writing has appeared in publications such as *MARGIE*, *decomP* and *Connotation Press*. She is the author of five poetry collections which include *An Amateur Marriage* (Finishing Line, 2012) as well as the award winning full length poetry collection, *Paper House* (Folded Word 2010). Her next collection, *MORPH*, will be released by Sibling Rivalry Press in the fall of 2013. Jessie is an adjunct instructor in the First-Year writing program at UNC-Charlotte. She is also the managing editor of *Referential Magazine*. She can be found around the web, especially at http://jessiecarty.com.

Justine Chan is a Chinese-American writer, poet and singer-songwriter from Chicago. She holds a B.A. in English and Creative Writing from University of Illinois at Urbana-Champaign. She was awarded an Undergraduate Creative Writing Award in 2010 and the Senior Quinn Creative Writing Award in 2011, both from the University of Illinois and for her fiction. She will be pursuing her MFA in Creative Writing from the University of Washington Seattle this fall. Her work also appears in *Storm Cellar* and *Midwestern Gothic*.

Lisa J. Cihlar's poems have appeared in *Blackbird*, *The South Dakota Review*, *Green Mountains Review*, *Crab Creek Review*, and *Southern Humanities Review*. She has been twice nominated for a Pushcart Prize. Her chapbook, *The Insomniac's House*, is available from Dancing Girl Press and a second chapbook, *This is How She Fails*, is available from Crisis Chronicles Press. She lives in rural southern Wisconsin.

Beth Copeland grew up in Japan, India, and North Carolina; her poems reflect a fusion between Eastern and Western themes and sensibilities. Her second book *Transcendental Telemarketer* (BlazeVOX books, 2012) received the runner up award in the North Carolina Poetry Council's 2013 Oscar Arnold Young Award for best poetry book by a North Carolina writer. Her first book *Traveling through Glass* received the 1999 Bright Hill Press Poetry Book Award. Two of her poems have been nominated for a Pushcart Prize. Copeland is an English instructor at Methodist University in Fayetteville, North Carolina. She lives with her husband Phil Rech in a log cabin in the country.

Kelly Cressio-Moeller's poetry has appeared or is forthcoming in *Valparaiso Poetry Review*, *Crab Orchard Review*, *Poet Lore*, *Crab Creek Review*, *Rattle*, *Boxcar Poetry Review*, *Gargoyle*, *The Sand Hill Review*, *Southern Humanities Review*, *Pearl*, *Switched-on Gutenberg*, *Melusine*, *Astropoetica*, and *The Newport Review*, among others. She lives in Northern California with her husband and two sons and is a reader on the editorial team of *Cæsura*. She's at work on her first book of poems.

Born in 1962, **Alison Croggon** is an Australian poet who writes in many genres, including criticism, theatre and prose. Her poetry has been published widely in anthologies and magazines in Australia and overseas. Her most recent poetry publication is *Theatre*, (Salt Publishing 2008). Others are *Ash* (Cusp Books, Los Angeles 2007), *November Burning* (Vagabond Press Rare Objects Series, Sydney, 2004); *Mnemosyne*, (Wild Honey Press, Ireland, 2001); *The Common Flesh (New and Selected Poems)* (Arc Publications, UK, 2003) and *Attempts at Being* (Salt Publishing, UK, 2002). She is also the author of the acclaimed young adult fantasy quartet, *The Books of Pellinor*, which has sold more than half a million copies worldwide. Her first book of poems, *This is the Stone*, won the 1991 Anne Elder and Dame Mary Gilmore Prizes. Her novel *Navigatio*, published by Black Pepper Press, was highly commended in the 1995 Australian/Vogel literary awards and is being translated for publication in France. Her second book of poems, *The Blue Gate*, was released in 1997 and was shortlisted for the Victorian Premier's Poetry Prize. *Attempts at Being* was shortlisted for the Kenneth Slessor Poetry Prize in the NSW Premier's Literary Awards and also was nominated for a Pushcart Prize in the US. Many of her poems have been set to music by various composers, including Smetanin. She is currently a regular columnist and poetry critic for *Overland* magazine. She was poetry editor for *Overland Extra* (1992), *Modern Writing* (1992-1994) and *Voices* (1996) and is founding editor of the literary arts journal *Masthead*.

Rachel Dacus' collections of poetry are the forthcoming *Gods of Water and Air*, *Earth Lessons*, *Femme au Chapeau*, and the spoken word CD *A God You Can Dance*. She has written on a variety of subjects, from travel in Italy to growing up a rocket kid in the race-to-space Cold War era. Her poems, stories, essays, reviews, and poet interviews have appeared in *Atlanta Review*, *Boulevard*, *Fringe Magazine*, *Many Mountains Moving*, *Prairie Schooner*, *Rattapallax*, and many other journals. She lives in Walnut Creek, California and raises funds for nonprofit organizations. Read more about her at http://racheldacus.net.

J. P. Dancing Bear is editor for the *American Poetry Journal* and Dream Horse Press; and hosts *Out of Our Minds* on public station, KKUP and available as podcasts. He is the author of twelve collections of poetry including, *Family of Marsupial Centaurs and other birthday poems* (Iris Press, 2012) and *The Abandoned Eye* (FutureCycle Press, 2012). His work has recently been translated and published in Chinese.

Yoko Danno is a Japanese poet, living in Kobe. She writes poetry solely in English. Many of her poems have appeared internationally in anthologies, magazines and online-journals. She is the author of several poetry books and chapbooks, including *Epitaph for memories* (The Bunny and the Crocodile Press, Washington, D.C., 2002), *The Blue Door*, a collaboration with James C. Hopkins (The Word Works, Washington, D.C., 2006), and *Trilogy & Hagoromo: A Celestial Robe* (The Ikuta Press, Kobe, 2010). Her English translation of Japanese myth and verse, *Songs and Stories of the Kojiki*, compiled in the 8th century, was published by Ahadada Books (Toronto/Tokyo, 2008). *a sleeping tiger dreams of manhattan: poetry, photographs and sound* by Danno, Hopkins, and Bernard Stoltz (The Ikuta Press, 2008) was translated into Latvian and published by Mansards (Riga, 2012). A new collection of her poems, *AQUAMARINE*, is forthcoming with Glass Lyre Press. Visit her at http://www.ikutapress.com/danno3.html/

Anannya Dasgupta is a poet and photographer. Her poetry and photography explore form and abstraction. Her poetry and artwork have appeared, among other places, at *Four Quarters Magazine, Wasafiri, OVS Magazine, Lantern Review, Asia Writes* and *Vox Poetica*. After earning a doctorate in Renaissance literature from Rutgers University, she now teaches in the department of English at St. Stephen's College, Delhi.

Lori Desrosiers has a book of poems, *The Philosopher's Daughter* (Salmon Poetry) and a chapbook, *Three Vanities* (Pudding House). Her poems have appeared in *New Millenium Review, Contemporary American Voices, BigCityLit, Concise Delights, Blue Fifth Review, Pirene's Fountain, The New Verse News, Common Ground Review*, and many more, including a prompt in *Wingbeats*, a book of writing exercises from Dos Gatos Press. Her MFA in Poetry is from New England College. She is editor and publisher of *Naugatuck River Review*, a journal of narrative poetry.

Teneice Durrant is the author of three chapbooks, most recently *Burden of Solace* (Cervena Barva 2012). She is a co-founder and poetry editor for *Blood Lotus: an online literary journal*, and the managing editor and publisher for Winged City Chapbook Press

Brian Fone For a decade and more after retiring early from lecturing in English Literature and Drama, Brian Fone owned and worked intermittently on a bush block on the Mid North Coast of New South Wales. The much loved flora and fauna of the area are the subjects of many of his poems.

Amy L. George is the author of two collections of poetry, *Desideratum* (Finishing Line Press, 2013) and *The Fragrance of Memory* (Amsterdam Press, 2009), as well as an online chapbook, *Sacred Fires and Ebullient Flames* (Red Ochre Press, 2011). Her poetry has been published in various journals, such as *Pirene's Fountain, WestWard Quarterly, The Foliate Oak Online, Toronto Quarterly, The Orange Room Review, Poesia* and others. She was also a contributor to *The Working Poet: 75 Writing Exercises and Poetry Anthology* (Autumn House Press, 2009). Recent works of hers have appeared in *PoetsArtists, Pennsylvania English* and *Kyoto Journal*. She holds an MFA in Creative Writing and is currently pursuing a Ph.D. in Literature and Criticism. She lives and teaches in Waxahachie, Texas.

Alex Grant's most recent collections are *The Poems of Wing Lei* and *The Circus Poems*. His poems have appeared in *The Missouri Review, Best New Poets 2007, Arts & Letters* and elsewhere. His work has received The Oscar Arnold Young Award, The Randall Jarrell Prize, The Pavel Srut Fellowship and the Kakalak Poetry Prize. A native Scot, he lives in Chapel Hill, NC, with his wife, his dangling participles and his Celtic fondness for excess.

Hedy Habra was born in Egypt and is of Lebanese origin. She is the author of a short story collection, *Flying Carpets*, a poetry collection, *Tea in Heliopolis*, and a book of literary criticism, *Mundos alternos y artísticos en Vargas Llosa*. She has an MA and an MFA in English and an MA and PhD in Spanish literature, all from Western Michigan University, where she currently teaches. She is the recipient of WMU's All-University Research and Creative Scholar Award. She writes poetry and fiction in French, Spanish, and English and her work has appeared in numerous journals and anthologies, including *Drunken Boat, Cutthroat, Nimrod, The Bitter Oleander, Puerto del Sol, The New York Quarterly, Cider Press Review, Poet Lore, Poetic Voices Without Borders 2, Inclined to Speak*, and *Dinarzad's Children Second Edition*. For more information, visit www.hedyhabra.com.

Until 2003, **David M. Harris** had never lived more than fifty miles from New York City. Since then he has moved to Tennessee, married, acquired a daughter and a classic MG, and gotten serious about poetry. All these projects seem to be working out pretty well. His work has also appeared in *Gargoyle, The Labletter, The Pedestal*, and other places. His first collection of poetry, *The ReviewMirror*, will come out from Unsolicited Press in the winter of 2013. On Sunday mornings, at 11 AM Central time, he talks about poetry on WRFN-LP in Pasquo, TN (www.radiofreenashville.org).

Mary Hutchins Harris is a poet and essayist. Her chapbook, *A Tongue Full of Yeses*, was selected by Kwame Dawes for publication in the South Carolina Poetry Initiative Chapbook Contest. She has been a featured poet for the Piccolo Spoleto Sundown Series and Stories for Life Festival in Charleston, SC and the South Carolina Book Festival. Her work appears in *American Athenaeum, Antietam Review, Kakalak, Main Street Rag, Pirene's Fountain, Poemeleon, Spillway, Tar River Poetry*, and *Waccamaw*, as well as in other print and on-line publications. She was the 2009 *Pirene's Fountain* Editors Award winner.

Melinda B Hipple is an award-winning writer, artist and photographer living in Kansas, USA. She writes in several different genre including short stories and novels. Among other publications, her published works have appeared in *Pirene's Fountain, Hillock, Prune Juice, Haijinx, Notes from the Gean, Tinywords, LYNX, The Buffalo Commons Storytelling Anthology*, and *Watershed*. In a past life she was a feature writer and monthly columnist for the outdoor sporting newspaper *Up the Creek News*. From September 2009 through June 2011, Melinda was haiga editor and web master for *Notes from the Gean*, a journal of Japanese short form poetry, and the guest editor of a Japanese short form poetry section for *Pirene's Fountain* in 2011. She was a founding member and haiga editor for *A Hundred Gourds*, a haikai poetry journal. Melinda has also won a number of poetry competitions, most recently the National Federation of State Poetry Society's 2013 Children's Poetry award.

Jane Hirshfield is the author of seven books of poetry, including *Come, Thief; After*, named a best book of 2006 by The Washington Post, The San Francisco Chronicle, and England's Financial Times; and *Given Sugar, Given Salt*, a finalist for the 2002 National Book Critics Circle Award. She is also the author of a book of essays, *Nine Gates: Entering the Mind of Poetry*, and has edited and co-translated four books bringing forward the work of world poets from the distant past. Her honors include fellowships from the NEA, the Academy of American Poets, and the Guggenheim and Rockefeller Foundations; Columbia University's Translation Center Award; and the California Book Award. Her work appears in *The New Yorker, The Atlantic, Poetry, Slate*, and seven editions of *The Best American Poetry*. She reads and lectures widely both in the US and internationally and is currently the Hellman Visiting Artist in the Neuroscience Department at UCSF. In 2012, she was named a Chancellor of the Academy of American Poets.

Paul Hostovsky is the author of four books of poetry and five poetry chapbooks. His poems have won a Pushcart Prize and two Best of the Net Awards. He has been featured on *Poetry Daily, Verse Daily*, and *The Writer's Almanac*. A new book of poems, *Naming*

Names, is forthcoming from Main Street Rag in fall/winter 2013. He works in Boston as an interpreter for the deaf. Visit him at www.paulhostovsky.com.

Marcia L. Hurlow is the author of five books of poems. The most recent are *Anomie* and *Green Man in Suburbia,* a collection of nature poems, including one that appeared originally in *Avocet.*

Larry Jordan's work has appeared in *Comstock Review, Pirene's Fountain, Red Savina Review, Straight Forward, Miller's Pond, Antiphon* and others. He is past editor for an online poetry forum and hails from South Carolina.

Robert S. King, a native Georgian, now lives in the mountains near Hayesville, NC. His poems appear in hundreds of magazines, including *California Quarterly, Chariton Review, Hollins Critic, Kenyon Review, Midwest Quarterly, Negative Capability, Southern Poetry Review,* and *Spoon River Poetry Review.* He has published three chapbooks (*When Stars Fall Down as Snow,* Garland Press 1976; *Dream of the Electric Eel,* Wolfsong Publications 1982; and *The Traveller's Tale,* Whistle Press 1998). His full-length collections are *The Hunted River* and *The Gravedigger's Roots,* both in 2nd editions from FutureCycle Press, 2012; and *One Man's Profit* from Sweatshoppe Publications, 2013.

Kathleen Kirk is the author of four poetry chapbooks, most recently *Nocturnes* (Hyacinth Girl Press, 2012). Her poems appear in many print and online journals, including *Blood Lotus, Blue Fifth Review, Confrontation, Eclectica,* and *Poems & Plays.* She is the poetry editor for *Escape Into Life.*

David LaBounty's work has appeared in *Rattle, the New Plains Review* and other journals. He is the author of the novel *Affluenza.* He lives in Michigan.

Rustin Larson's poetry has appeared in *The New Yorker, The Iowa Review, North American Review, Poetry East, Saranac Review, Poets/Artists* and other magazines. He is the author of *The Wine-Dark House* (Blue Light Press, 2009) and *Crazy Star* (selected for the Loess Hills Book's Poetry Series in 2005). Larson won 1st Editor's Prize from *Rhino* magazine in 2000 and has won prizes for his poetry from The National Poet Hunt and The Chester H. Jones Foundation among others. A seven-time Pushcart nominee, and graduate of the Vermont College MFA in Writing, Larson was an Iowa Poet at The Des Moines National Poetry Festival in 2002 & 2004, a featured writer in the DMACC Celebration of the Literary Arts in 2007 & 2008, and he was a featured poet at the Poetry at Round Top [Texas] Festival in May 2012. His latest collection, *Bum Cantos, Winter Jazz, & The Collected Discography of Morning,* won the 2013 Blue Light Book Award (Blue Light Press, San Francisco).

Dorianne Laux's most recent books of poetry are *The Book of Men,* winner of the Paterson Poetry Prize, and *Facts about the Moon,* recipient of the Oregon Book Award and short-listed for the Lenore Marshall Poetry Prize. Laux is also author of *Awake, What We Carry,* finalist for the National Book Critic's Circle Award, and *Smoke.* She teaches poetry and directs the MFA program at North Carolina State University and she is founding faculty at Pacific University's Low Residency MFA Program.

Lyn Lifshin's *Another Woman Who Looks Like Me* was published by Black Sparrow at David Godine October, 2006.. (Also out in 2006 is her prize winning book about the famous, short lived beautiful race horse, Ruffian: *The Licorice Daughter: My Year With Ruffian* from Texas Review Press. Lifshin's other recent books include *Before it's Light* published winter 1999-2000 by Black Sparrow press, following their publication of *Cold Comfort* in 1997 and *92 Rapple* from Coatism.: *Lost in the*

Fog and *Barbaro: Beyond Brokeness* and *Light at the End, the Jesus Poems, Katrina, Ballet Madonnas*. For other books, bio, photographs see her web site: www.lynlifshin.com *Persephone* was published by Red Hen and Texas Review published *Barbaro: Beyond Brokenness*. Most recent books: *Ballroom, All the Poets (Mostly) Who Have Touched me, Living and Dead. All True, Especially the Lies*. And just out, *Knife Edge & Absinthe: The Tango Poems* and *Hitchcock Hotel*. In Spring 2012, NYQ books published *A Girl Goes into The Woods*. Also just published: *For the Roses* poems after Joni Mitchell. Forthcoming books include *Secretariat: The Red Freak, The Miracle*, and *The Malala Poems, The Tangled Alphabet: Istanbul Poems*. A DVD of her film *Lyn Lifshin: Not Made of Glass* is now available.

Aine MacAodha is a writer and Photographer from Omagh situated North of Ireland. Her recent works have appeared in, Doghouse Anthology of Irish haiku titled, *Bamboo Dreams, Poethead Blog, Glasgow Review, Enniscorthy Echo*, wordsocialforum, previous published poems translated into Italian and Turkish, honourable mention in *Diogen pro culture winter Haiku contest, thefirscut* issues #6 and #7, *Outburst magazine*, celticburialrites.blogspot.co.uk *A New Ulster* issues 2 and 4, *Pirene's Fountain Japanese Short Form Issue, Peony Moon, DIOGEN pro culture magazine world poetry day*, Poetry broadcast on '*Words on Top*' radio show. She has published two volumes of poetry, '*Where the Three rivers Meet*' and *Guth An Anam (Voice of the soul)*. Her photographic work has also appeared in, http://lightonthepage.com/, wordsocialforum, http://www.thewildgeesegenealogy.blogspot.ie/2012/05/making-art-by-ulsters-sperrins-q-with.html

Amy MacLennan has been published in *Hayden's Ferry Review, River Styx, Linebreak, Cimarron Review, Painted Bride Quarterly, Folio*, and *Rattle*. Her chapbook, *The Fragile Day*, was released from Spire Press in the summer of 2011, and her chapbook, *Weathering*, was published by Uttered Chaos Press in early 2012. She has a poem appearing in the anthology *Myrrh, Mothwing, Smoke: Erotic Poems* that was published by Tupelo Press in March 2013

Dennis Maloney is the editor and publisher of the widely respected White Pine Press in Buffalo, NY which will celebrate its 40th year in 2013. He is also a poet and translator. His works of translation include: *The Stones of Chile* by Pablo Neruda, *The Landscape of Castile* by Antonio Machado, *Between the Floating Mist: Poems of Ryokan, Tangled Hair: Tanka of Yosano Akiko* and *The Poet and the Sea* by Juan Ramon Jimenez. A number of volumes of his own poetry have been published including *The Map Is Not the Territory: Poems & Translations* and *Just Enough*.

David McAleavey's fifth and most recent book is *HUGE HAIKU* (317 pp., Chax Press, Tucson, 2005), and he has had poems in *Poetry, Ploughshares*, and *The Georgia Review*. Since 2010, he has had over a hundred poems accepted for publication, both in print and online, in such places as *Poetry Northwest, Denver Quarterly, Hubbub, Poet Lore, Connecticut Review, Hampden-Sydney Poetry Review, Memoir (and)*, Anon (U.K.), *Limestone, Magma Poetry* (U.K.), *Chiron Review, diode poetry journal, DMQ Review, Rougarou, Medulla Review, Ascent, Eclectica, Innisfree, Pedestal, White Whale Review, Praxilla, Waccamaw, Stand* (U.K.), *Epoch, Poetry East, American Letters & Commentary*, and *Anderbo.com*. *Pirene's Fountain* awarded him their 2011-12 Editor's Prize for best poem. *New Delta Review* has published work of his in their 2013 "Best of the Web" anthology. He teaches literature and creative writing at George Washington University in Washington, DC.

Michelle McGrane's collection *The Suitable Girl* is published by Pindrop Press in the United Kingdom and Modjaji Books in South Africa. She lives in Johannesburg and is a member of SA PEN. Visit *Peony Moon*, her contemporary poetry blog, at http://peonymoon.wordpress.com

Catherine McGuire is a writer and artist with a deep interest in philosophy, the "Why are we here?" question that lurks under so much of our lives. Using nature as a mirror, she explores the way humans perceive themselves and their world. She has had almost 300 poems published in venues such as: *Adagio, Avocet, Folio, Fireweed, FutureCycle, Green Fuse, Main Street Rag, New Verse News, Nibble, Portland Lights Anthology* and *Tapjoe*. Her chapbook, *Palimpsests*, was released by Uttered Chaos in 2011. She has three self-published chapbooks: *Joy Holding Stillness, Poetry and Chickens*, and *Glimpses of a Garden*. Her website is www.cathymcguire.com.

Steve Meador has three books of poetry published and when he is not on a road trip you can find him in Florida working as a real estate broker. His work appears regularly in print and online journals. Since he is too humble to provide a long list, you can google him. The truly uninterested follower can catch Steve's rants and ramblings, when he feels the need to post, at: http://thedisgruntledwriter.blogspot.com/

Corey Mesler has published in numerous journals and anthologies. He has published seven novels, 3 full length poetry collections, and 3 books of short stories. He has also published over a dozen chapbooks of both poetry and prose. He has been nominated for the Pushcart Prize numerous times, and two of his poems have been chosen for Garrison Keillor's Writer's Almanac. His fiction has received praise from John Grisham, Robert Olen Butler, Lee Smith, Frederick Barthelme, Greil Marcus, among others. With his wife, he runs Burke's Book Store in Memphis TN, one of the country's oldest (1875) and best independent bookstores. He can be found at www.coreymesler.wordpress.com.

Joseph Millar's three collections are *Overtime, Fortune*, and *Blue Rust* (2012 Carnegie-Mellon). Millar grew up in Pennsylvania, attended the Johns Hopkins Writing Seminars and spent 30 years in the San Francisco Bay area working at a variety of jobs, from telephone repairman to commercial fisherman. It would be two decades before he returned to poetry. His poems record the narrative of a life fully lived among fathers, sons, brothers, daughters, weddings and divorces, men and women. His work has won fellowships from the Guggenheim Foundation, the National Endowment for the Arts and a 2008 Pushcart Prize and has appeared in such magazines as *DoubleTake, TriQuarterly, The Southern Review, American Poetry Review*, and *Ploughshares*. Millar is now core faculty at Pacific University's Low Residency MFA and lives in Raleigh, NC, with his wife, the poet Dorianne Laux.

Sue Millard, known on several writing web sites as 'Fellpony', was allowed to "stand up close to a horse" at the age of two and a half and has not been the same since… She has written quite a bit for equestrian magazines over the years and had several books published including *Hoofprints in Eden*, an award-winning examination of the Fell Pony's background and history (Hayloft , 2005). Since retiring from her post as a university lecturer in 2009, Sue has published three more novels and is working on two others (details of her catalogue can be found at http://www.jackdawebooks.co.uk/). A poetry pamphlet, *Ash Tree*, is in press with Prole Books and due out August 2013. Sue is married with two grown kids, one of each. (Her curiosity satisfied!) She lives on a small farm in Cumbria with husband Graham, sheepdog Sammy, and her two Fell ponies.

Suchoon Mo is a Korean War veteran and a retired academic living in the semiarid part of Colorado. His poems and music compositions appeared in a number of literary and cultural publications. His recent poetry chapbook, *Frog Mantra*, has been published by Accents Publications of Lexington, Kentucky.

Jim Moore's *New and Selected Poems* will be available from Graywolf Press in September, 2014. He is a 2012 recipient of a Guggenheim Fellowship in Poetry. He lives in Minneapolis, Minnesota and in Spoleto, Italy with his wife the photographer, JoAnn Verburg.

Karen Neuberg lives and writes in Brooklyn, NY and West Hurley, NY. Her work appears or is forthcoming in the anthologies *Child of My Child*, *Hudson Valley Women Writers*, and *Riverine* as well as in online and print journals including *Barrow Street*, *DIAGRAM*, *Levure Litterature*, *Melusine, or Woman in the 21st Century*, *Nassau Review*, and *Poets for Living Waters*. Her chapbook, *Detailed Still*, was published by Poets Wear Prada. She's a five-time Pushcart and a Best of the Net nominee, holds an MFA from the New School, and is associate editor of *First Literary Review-East*. When not writing poetry, she enjoys spending time with family and friends, practicing tai chi and yoga, hiking, gardening, and traveling. Links to her work can be found at www.karenneuberg.blogspot.com

Aimee Nezhukumatathil is the author of three books of poetry, most recently, *LUCKY FISH*. Awards for her work include an NEA fellowship and the Pushcart Prize. She is professor of English at SUNY-Fredonia.

Scott Owens' tenth collection of poetry, *Shadows Trail Them Home*, was recently published by Clemson University Press. His prior work has received awards from the Academy of American Poets, the Pushcart Prize Anthology, the Next Generation/Indie Lit Awards, the NC Writers Network, the NC Poetry Society, and the Poetry Society of SC. He is the founder of Poetry Hickory, editor of Wild Goose Poetry Review and 234, and vice president of the NC Poetry Society. Born and raised in Greenwood, SC, he currently teaches at Catawba Valley Community College in Hickory, NC.

Linda Pastan was born in New York City, graduated from Radcliffe College and received an MA from Brandeis University. Her awards a Pushcart Prize, the Di Castagnola Award (Poetry Society of America), the Bess Hokin Prize (Poetry Magazine), the Maurice English Award, the Charity Randall Citation of the International Poetry Forum, and the 2003 Ruth Lilly Poetry Prize. She was a recipient of a Radcliffe College Distinguished Alumnae Award. *PM/AM* and *Carnival Evening* were nominees for the National Book Award and *The Imperfect Paradise* was a nominee for the Los Angeles Times Book Prize. She served as Poet Laureate of Maryland from 1991 to 1995 and was on the staff of the Breadloaf Writers Conference for twenty years. She lives in Potomac, Maryland.

Connie Post served as the first Poet Laureate of Livermore, California from 2005 - 2009. Her work has appeared in *The Aurorean*, *Calyx*, *Kalliope*, *Barnwood International*, *Cold Mountain Review*, *Crab Creek Review*, *Comstock Review*, *DMQ Review*, *Dogwood*, *Iodine Poetry Journal*, *Main Street Rag*, *The Great American Poetry Show*, *Karamu*, *Pirene's Fountain*, *Psychic Meatloaf*, *The Pedestal Magazine*, *Up The Staircase*, *Slipstream*, *Wild Goose Poetry Review*, and *The Toronto Quarterly*. She was the winner of the Cover Prize for the Spring 2009 issue of *The Dirty Napkin* and the winner of the 2009 Caesura Poetry Awards from Poetry Center of San Jose. Her 2012 Chapbook from Finishing Line Press *And When the Sun Drops* won the Fall Aurorean 2012 Editor's Choice award. She is a four time Pushcart nominee. Her first full length collection *Flood Water* will be released in late 2013 from Glass Lyre Press.

Doug Ramspeck is the author of four poetry collections. His most recent book, *Mechanical Fireflies* (2011) received the Barrow Street Press Poetry Prize. His first book, *Black Tupelo Country* (BkMk Press, 2008), received the John Ciardi Prize for Poetry. His poems have appeared in journals that include *Slate*, *The Kenyon Review*, *The Southern Review*, *The Georgia Review*, *Alaska Quarterly Review*, *AGNI*, and *Prairie Schooner*. He is the recipient of an Ohio Arts Council Individual Excellence Award. He teaches creative writing and directs the Writing Center at The Ohio State University at Lima.

Mary Kay Rummel is the author of two poetry chapbooks and four full length collections. Blue Light Press of San Francisco published *What's Left Is The Singing* in 2010 and will publish *The Lifeline Trembles* in 2014. Mary Kay is a recipient of four Pushcart nominations. Her poems recently won first prize in the poetry contests sponsored by Irish-American Crossroads of San Francisco and by Ventura County Writers' Club. Dividing her time between Minneapolis and Ventura, she performs poetry with musicians and dancers and teaches part time at California State University, Channel Islands. Her poems have appeared in numerous journals and anthologies, most recently in the 2013 *Nimrod* Awards issue, *The Whirlwind Review*, and the anthologies *Daring to Repair* (Wising Up Press) and *The Heart of All That Is: Reflections on Home* (Holy Cow! Press.) www.marykayrummel.com

C. J. Sage edits *The National Poetry Review* and The National Poetry Review Press. Her poems have appeared in *Antioch Review, Barrow Street, Black Warrior Review, Boston Review, Conduit, the Literary Review, Orion, Ploughshares, Shenandoah, The Threepenny Review*, etc. Her latest book is *The San Simeon Zebras* (Salmon, 2010) and her next book, *Open House*, is forthcoming from Salmon in 2014. C. J. resides in Rio Del Mar, California, where she works as a Realtor and a visual artist.

Rebecca Seiferle was named Tucson Poet Laureate in 2012. Recently her work was selected for *Streetscapes*, a public art project in Phoenix Arizona. Her most recent poetry collection, *Wild Tongue*, (Copper Canyon Press, 2007) won the 2008 Grub Street National Poetry Prize. She has three previous poetry collections: *Bitters* (Copper Canyon, 2001) won the Western States Book Award and a Pushcart prize; *The Music We Dance To* (Sheep Meadow Press, 1998) won the Hemley Award from the Poetry Society of America; *The Ripped-Out Seam* (Sheep Meadow Press, 1993) won the Bogin Memorial Award, The National Writer's Union Prize, and the Poets & Writers Exchange Award. In 2004 she was awarded a poetry fellowship from the Lannan Foundation. She is a noted translator: Copper Canyon Press published her translation of Vallejo's *The Black Heralds* in 2003. She is the Founding Editor of the online international poetry journal *The Drunken Boat* (http://www.thedrunkenboat.com). She has taught at the Summer Literary Seminars in Vilnius, the Provincetown Fine Arts Center, Key West Literary Seminar, Port Townsend Writer's Conference, Gemini Ink, the Stonecoast MFA program, and was Jacob Ziskind poet-in-residence at Brandeis University. She currently lives in Tucson, Arizona and teaches at Southwest University of Visual Arts. Visit her at http://www.thedrunkenboat.com/seiferle.htm

John Siddique is the author of six books, the most recent of which is *Full Blood*. His poetry, essays and articles have featured in *Granta, The Guardian, Poetry Review, The Rialto* and on BBC Radio 4. Jackie Kay speaks of Siddique's writing as being 'A brilliant balancing act.' Siddique is the former British Council Writer-in-Residence at California State University, Los Angeles. Think-Tank QED considers John to be one of the 21 most influential people in the UK with South Asian heritage. John is the Royal Literary Fund Fellow at York St. John's University and was recently awarded the title of Honorary Creative Writing Fellow by the University of Leicester in recognition of his contribution to literature.

Jeffrey Side has had poetry published in various magazines such as *Poetry Salzburg Review* and on poetry websites such as *Underground Window, A Little Poetry, Poethia, Nthposition, Eratio, Pirene's Fountain, Fieralingue, Moria, Ancient Heart, Blazevox, Lily,*

Big Bridge, Jacket, Textimagepoem, Apochryphaltext, 9th St. Laboratories, P. F. S. Post, Great Works, Hutt, The Dande Review, Poetry Bay and *Dusie*. He has reviewed poetry for *Jacket, Eyewear, The Colorado Review, New Hope International, Stride, Acumen* and *Shearsman*. From 1996 to 2000 he was the deputy editor of *The Argotist* magazine, and is currently the editor of the online successor of this, *The Argotist Online*, which has an ebook publishing arm called Argotist Ebooks. His publications include *Carrier of the Seed, Slimvol, Distorted Reflections, Cyclones in High Northern Latitudes* (with Jake Berry) and *Outside Voices: An Email Correspondence* (with Jake Berry).

The author of fourteen books, **Judith Skillman's** latest poetry collection is *The Phoenix: New & Selected Poems 2007 – 2013*, from Dream Horse Press. The recipient of funding from the Academy of American Poets for her book *Storm* (Blue Begonia Press), she has received a King County Arts Commission (KCAC) Publication Prize and other awards. *Broken Lines—The Art & Craft of Poetry* is just out from Lummox Press (www.lummoxpress.com). Skillman's poems and collaborative translations have appeared in *Poetry, FIELD, The Southern Review, The Iowa Review, Midwest Quarterly Review, Ezra, Prairie Schooner, Seneca Review*, and numerous other journals and anthologies. She has been a Writer in Residence at the Centrum Foundation in Port Townsend, Washington, and Hedgebrook in Langley, Washington. A Jack Straw Writer in 2008 and 2013, her work has been nominated for Pushcart Prizes, the UK Kit Award, Best of the Web, and is included in *Best Indie Verse of New England*. Judith Skillman was born in Syracuse NY of Canadian parents, and holds dual citizenship. She is an amateur violinist, the mother of three grown children, and the "Grammy" of twin girls. Visit www.judithskillman.com

Craig Colin Smith lives in Salt Lake City where he works as a technical writer in education technology. Craig's poetry has appeared in various print and online publications including *Pirene's Fountain*, which awarded him the 2010 Editor's prize for his poem "Song of Oak." Craig was also a featured poet for the Library of Congress's Poetry at Noon series. He is working on a collection of poetry and a series of essays on aesthetics.

Four time Pushcart Prize nominee **J.R. Solonche** has been publishing in magazines, journals, and anthologies since the early 70s. He is coauthor of *Peach Girl: Poems for a Chinese Daughter* (Grayson Books) and author of the forthcoming *Beautiful Day* from Deerbrook Editions. He lives in New York's Hudson Valley.

Joannie Stangeland's third book of poems, *Into the Rumored Spring*, was published by Ravenna Press. She's also the author of two poetry chapbooks— *Weathered Steps* and *A Steady Longing for Flight*, which won the Floating Bridge Press Chapbook Award. Joannie's poems have appeared in *Superstition Review, Tulane Review, Valparaiso Poetry Review, Fire On Her Tongue*, and other publications and anthologies, as well as on the bus. Joannie helps edit the online journals *The Smoking Poet* and *Cascadia Review*.

Tim Suermondt is the author of two full-length collections: *Trying to Help the Elephant Man Dance* (The Backwaters Press, 2007) and *Just Beautiful* from New York Quarterly Books, 2010. He has published poems in *Poetry, The Georgia Review, Blackbird, Able Muse, Prairie Schooner, PANK, Bellevue Literary Review* and *Stand Magazine* (U.K.) and has poems forthcoming in Gargoyle, A Narrow Fellow and DMQ Review among others. After many years in Queens and Brooklyn, he has moved to Cambridge with his wife, the poet Pui Ying Wong.

Maria Terrone is the author of the poetry collections *A Secret Room in Fall* (McGovern Award, Ashland Poetry Press) and *The Bodies We Were Loaned* (The Word Works) as well as a chapbook, *American Gothic, Take 2* (Finishing Line Press). Her third collection, *Eye to Eye*, is forthcoming from Bordighera Press in 2014. Her work, which has been translated into French and Farsi and nominated four times for a Pushcart Award, has appeared in magazines including *Poetry, Ploughshares, Hudson Review*, and *Poetry International*. She was one of 10 Queens-based writers commissioned in Spring 2012 by the Guggenheim Museum for its project, "sillspotting nyc." Visit her at www.mariaterrone.com

K.J. Van Deusen's poems can be found in *mediterranean poetry, Plain Spoke: A Literary Speakeasy, Eunoia Review, Victorian Violet Press and Journal, Granite Island, Amber Sea: Writings from the Black Hills and Plains*, and several issues of *Pirene's Fountain*. At the time of this printing, she is pulling up deep Black Hills of South Dakota roots and heading for the Pacific Ocean and a new life on its rugged and gorgeous edge.

Marc Vincenz is Swiss-British, was born in Hong Kong, and currently divides his time between Reykjavik and New York City. His work has appeared in many journals, including *Washington Square Review, Fourteen Hills, The Potomac, Saint Petersburg Review, The Canary, Spillway, The Bitter Oleander*, and *Guernica*. Recent collections include: *The Propaganda Factory, or Speaking of Trees* (2011); *Gods of a Ransacked Century* (2013) and *Mao's Mole* (Neopoiesis Press, 2013). A new English-German bi-lingual collection, *Additional Breathing Exercises / Zusätzliche Atemübungen*, is forthcoming from Wolfbach Verlag, Zurich, Switzerland (2014).

Jane Yolen's books and stories have won an assortment of awards--two Nebulas, a World Fantasy Award, a Caldecott, the Golden Kite Award, three Mythopoeic awards, two Christopher Medals, a nomination for the National Book Award, and the Jewish Book Award, among others. She is also the winner (for body of work) of the Kerlan Award, the World Fantasy Assn. Lifetime Achievement Award, Science Fiction Poetry Association Grand Master Award, the Catholic Library's Regina Medal, and the 2012 du Grummond Medal. Six colleges and universities have given her honorary doctorates. Also worthy of note, her Skylark Award—given by NESFA, the New England Science Fiction Association, set her good coat on fire. If you need to know more about her, visit her website at: www.janeyolen.com

Desmond Kon Zhicheng-Mingdé is the author of *I Didn't Know Mani Was A Conceptualist*, forthcoming in 2013. He has also edited more than ten books and co-produced three audio books, some edited pro bono for non-profit organizations. These titles span the genres of ethnography, journalism, creative nonfiction, and corporate literature. A former entertainment journalist with *8 Days*, Desmond has traveled to Australia, France, Hong Kong and Spain for his stories, which have included features on Madonna, Björk and Morgan Freeman, culminating in the authorship of the limited edition *Top Ten TCS Stars* for Caldecott Publishing. Trained in book publishing at Stanford University, Desmond studied sociology and mass communication at the National University of Singapore, and later received his Theology masters (World Religions) from Harvard University and Fine Arts masters (Creative Writing) from the University of Notre Dame. An interdisciplinary artist, Desmond also works in clay, his ceramic works housed in museums and private collections in India, the Netherlands, the United Kingdom, and the United States. He is the recipient of the PEN American Center Shorts Prize, Swale Life Poetry Prize, Cyclamens & Swords Poetry Prize, Stepping Stones Nigeria Poetry Prize, and Little Red Tree International Poetry Prize, among other awards.

Editors

Steve Asmussen grew up in Chicagoland, and has a degree in Electronics and Computer Technology. He loves to read and write and cook — sometimes all three at once. He is the associate layout editor for Glass Lyre Press. *First Water* is the second published book he has laid out, though his first with Glass Lyre. He currently lives in Des Plaines, Illinois.

Royce Hamel is a cum laude graduate of Columbia College Chicago with a B.A. in Fiction Writing. She is a freelance writer and novelist. When not writing, she reviews and edits for Glass Lyre Press & *Pirene's Fountain*, and she is currently working on several novels involving sci-fi, fantasy, and survival at all costs.

Katherine Herschler is the design and layout editor for Glass Lyre Press. She manages the *Pirene's Fountain* website and layout for the Glass Lyre books. Katherine designed the book cover and interior for *Sunrise from Blue Thunder*. She is a graduate of The Illinois Institute of Art, Schaumburg for Interior Design, and currently works as an Associate Interior Designer at an architectural firm in the Chicagoland area. Katherine has won several well-deserved staff awards of excellence from *Pirene's Fountain*.

Ami Kaye is the publisher and managing editor of Glass Lyre Press and *Pirene's Fountain*. Various literary journals and anthologies have published her work, and she is the author of *What Hands Can Hold*. Visit amikaye.com

Mark McKay is the editor-in-chief of Glass Lyre Press, and has been on the editing team of *Pirene's Fountain* from the outset. An avid reader, Mark has written poetry, review features and author interviews. Mark's first love was the lyrical poetry of his native land: Burns, McDiarmid, MacKay Brown and Muir. These days he enjoys literature of all kinds and from all corners of the globe.

Elizabeth Nichols is a graduate of Roosevelt University with a B.A. in English Literature. She is a data entry representative for Volkswagen Credit, and writes and edits in her spare time. When not working as Associate Editor for Glass Lyre Press & *Pirene's Fountain*, Elizabeth indulges in her passions for libraries, museums, and old time radio and classic cinema. She looks forward to brandishing her red editor's pen proudly for the GLP team.

Lark Vernon Timmons is the editor-in-chief of *Pirene's Fountain*. She is a native Texan, born and raised in the beautiful desert Southwest. She has a lifelong love and respect for written language, influenced by her grandfather, a newspaper editor for the *Kansas City Star*, and her father, a well-respected local historian and author. Lark has been on the editing team of *Pirene's Fountain* since its inception in 2008. She considers it a privilege to be a part of PF's newest venture, Glass Lyre Press publishing.

Artist

Tracy McQueen is a freelance artist who has worked with *Pirene's Fountain* from its inception in 2008. In addition to her art and design work for *Pirene's Fountain*, she has created four book covers and illustrated three books including *Sunrise from Blue Thunder*. She has received her Bachelor of Fine Arts degree from The American Academy of Art, Chicago, and focuses mainly on digital media.

GLASS LYRE PRESS, LLC
"Exceptional works to replenish the spirit"

Poetry Collections
Poetry Chapbooks
Select Short & Flash Fiction
Occasional Anthologies

Glass Lyre Press is a small independent literary press interested in work which is technically accomplished and distinctive in style, as well as fresh in its approach and treatment. Glass Lyre seeks writers of diverse backgrounds who display mastery over the many areas of contemporary literature, writers with a powerful and dynamic aesthetic, and ability to stir the imagination and engage the emotions and intellect of a wide audience of readers.

The Glass Lyre vision is to connect the world through language and art. We hope to expand the scope of poetry and short fiction for the general reader through exceptionally well-written books which call forth our deepest emotions and thoughts, delight our senses, challenge our minds, and provide clarity, resonance and insight.

www.GlassLyrePress.com

www.ingramcontent.com/pod-product-compliance
Lightning Source LLC
Chambersburg PA
CBHW020651300426
44112CB00007B/331